THE FEASTS OF ISRAEL

ISRAEL'S JOURNEY IN CHRIST TOWARDS GOD'S ULTIMATE END

BY JASON R. HENDERSON

**This and other publications
are available <u>FREE</u> upon request
by contacting:**

Market Street Fellowship
981 W. Market Street   Akron, Ohio 44311
email: MSFPrinting@gmail.com
phone: 330-419-1527

v.2

Contents

Preface

This book is a re-written and expanded version of an outline that was originally used for a conference in Ohio in December of 2011.   In the words of Paul, I offer this book "in weakness, in fear, and in much trembling," very aware of my ability to nullify the grace of God by offering the Lord's body something of myself, my flesh, my own ideas. The reader is therefore asked to bear in mind that the things presented in this book represent my *current* view of the seven feasts of Israel, which is, without question, a very limited view.   My understanding of the feasts is, most certainly, a work in progress.

I would recommend that this *not* be the first book you read of those offered by Market Street Fellowship.   There are statements made and important topics referenced that are not well explained or supported here because they have been dealt with at length elsewhere.   The realities described in this book rest securely upon an understanding of the finished work of the cross, which is described in our publication *Not I, But Christ,* as well as in many other resources available on our website.

```
┌─────────────────────────────────────────────────────────┐
│                 THE FEASTS OF ISRAEL                      │
│     Spring Feasts                          Fall Feasts    │
│                                                           │
│     Passover        50 days      120 days    Trumpets     │
│         |                                        |        │
│  Unleavened Bread ──→ Pentecost ──→ Day of Atonement      │
│         |                                        |        │
│     First Fruits                            Tabernacles   │
└─────────────────────────────────────────────────────────┘
```

Chapter I
General Information

The word translated "feast" in the Bible is actually the Hebrew word *mo'ed*. Translating *mo'ed* as feast can be misleading because for many the word feast implies a great meal, often accompanied by some sort of celebration. While it is true that some of the feasts of Israel involved meals and celebration, the word *mo'ed* actually means *"appointed place, appointed time, appointed meeting"*[1] and the purpose of a *mo'ed* was to signify something, or to act as a sign. Perhaps the words "convocation" or "assembly" would more accurately communicate the meaning of this Hebrew word.

The purpose for these seven annual assemblies was not primarily eating or celebrating. The purpose was to paint a picture representing God's perspective of His work and purpose in a specific way, at a specific time, for a specific reason. Generally speaking, I believe the feasts represent

---

[1]   Strong's Exhaustive Bible Concordance # H 4150

the work and purpose of the Lord in Christ, and our inclusion with Him in His work, and for His purpose, with all that that entails.

Because the feasts are intricately tied to the land and the harvest (and therefore things like planting, cultivating, increase, seasons, and ultimately reaping), it seems clear that the Lord is demonstrating a process, an order, a goal, and an increase unto an objective. In other words, the feasts start somewhere, go in a particular direction, and reach an intentional objective. They are not seven random types and shadows. There is an order to them, and the order is important.

They begin with the death, burial, and resurrection of Jesus Christ, represented in the first three feasts. These first feasts represent the finished work of salvation through the cross of Christ and they are connected to barley, the first crop in Israel's yearly harvest. Fifty days later, a corporate people are made to participate in this finished work. Israel (made up of Jew and Gentile) is baptized into Christ at Pentecost and is carried along towards Tabernacles, also called the Feast of the Ingathering. All of this will be discussed in detail, but the important thing for now is to recognize an intentional order that represents Israel's journey in Christ towards God's ultimate end.

The feasts were an enormous part of old covenant Judaism, and the yearly experience of these feasts, together with their corresponding harvests, were critical aspects of every Jew's personal, social, and spiritual identity. Jesus often used feast language in His parables, and His listeners certainly would have recognized and understood these references. For example, He connected His work and purpose with a harvest or increase, beginning with the wheat harvest.

> ***Matt 13:30*** *Let both grow together until the harvest, and at the time of harvest I will say to the reapers, "First gather together the tares and bind them in bundles to burn them, but gather the wheat into my barn." (NKJV)*

This verse ties the wheat harvest to a gathering and a judgment at the end of the old covenant age. As James says, the apostle's generation of believers were "a kind of firstfruits of His creatures."[2] Once we are familiar with the seven feasts, it is interesting to begin to notice how often the language of the feasts (seed, increase, harvest, reaper, etc) appears throughout the gospels and the letters of the New Testament.

Like with all of the types and shadows of the old covenant, the coming of the Messiah brought the fulfillment and substance of each one of the seven feasts. Jesus was not randomly selecting feast-language when He taught the multitudes and told His parables. Jesus was gathering up the God-given pictures within the feasts of Israel, and declaring Himself to be their fulfillment.

> ***John 4:34*** *Jesus said to them, "My food is to do the will of Him who sent Me, and to finish His work. 35 Do you not say, 'There are still four*

---

[2]   James 1:18

months and then comes the harvest'? Behold, I say to you, lift up your eyes and look at the fields, for they are already white for harvest! 36 And he who reaps receives wages, and gathers fruit for eternal life, that both he who sows and he who reaps may rejoice together. 37 For in this the saying is true: 'One sows and another reaps.' 38 I sent you to reap that for which you have not labored; others have labored, and you have entered into their labors."

Here again, the feast-language is impossible to miss. There were four months between Pentecost and the final feasts in the seventh month. During that time Israel gathered up the increase that was given to them by God. Here in John 4, Jesus is the one sowing Himself (the Word that came from God) into the hearts of all who would receive Him. The apostles would be the first ones to reap the increase of Christ in the new Israel, and both Sower and reapers would rejoice together as one.

In verses like these we can see the reality of the process, order, and goal that was mentioned above. The feasts were not random celebrations. They were intricately tied to the agricultural season in Israel, and therefore represent the journey of Christ from a single dying seed to a multi-membered, resurrected harvest.

Manifestation vs. Fulfillment

Each of the feasts had some sort of expression or manifestation in the earth that can be linked to them. Nevertheless, we must never confuse manifestation with fulfillment. Physical manifestation always testifies of, or witnesses to, the fulfillment. The fulfillment, however, is Christ, is *in* Christ, and therefore also works in us by Christ. God has never promised or prophesied anything that will find its fulfillment outside the boundaries of Jesus Christ. In other words, a natural event or a physical thing could never contain the substance of what God was testifying to through His types and shadows, promises and prophecies. The spirit of prophecy is the testimony of Jesus Himself and not anything external to Him.

Therefore, the true fulfillment of each of these feasts is an inward, spiritual, eternal experience of Christ and is not tied to natural events (future or past) except for the purpose of manifestation or illustration. To give one example, we see a great *manifestation* of Pentecost in Acts chapter two. This was the day where God poured out His Spirit on the body of Christ. There were signs (wind, tongues of fire) and miracles (languages, healings) that accompanied this outpouring. But you cannot say that Pentecost was fulfilled on that one day, 2000 years ago. Pentecost is not an *event* that came and went in the first century. It is not bound by time. The fulfillment of Pentecost is a spiritual, eternal, and inward experience of every single believer. It had natural manifestations then and may have natural manifestations now, but the *fulfillment* is the timeless gift of God's Spirit that now lives and works in the body of Christ.

Unfortunately, the great majority of modern authors who write about the feasts argue that the fulfillment of all seven are found in physical events, and in nearly every case the last three are said to be still future events. It would not matter to me if these authors were describing merely a future *manifestation* of the feasts through natural events, yet understanding their *fulfillment* to be spiritual, timeless, in Christ, and as Christ. But seeking the fulfillment of the feasts in future events implies that these realities are currently unavailable to the believer.

Overview of the Seven Feasts

In a very general way, I would summarize the feasts as follows: the first three represent the foundation; the fourth establishes the relationship; the last three represent the purpose or consummation towards which God brings the relationship.

Every one of the feasts is tied to the cross and the believer's experience of all that God accomplished there. We never move beyond any of the feasts. But coming to know each of them in the person of Christ, we grow towards God's eternal purpose, towards the "measure of the stature of the fullness of Christ."[3]

---

[3]   Ephesians 4:13

The feasts of Passover, Unleavened Bread, and Firstfruits testify of the objective, perfected, finished work of Christ through death, burial, and resurrection. Keeping the feast (i.e. when Israel does the things required by the Lord at the appointed times) has to do with the believer's acceptance, participation in, and experience of this perfect work. Christ completed each of these three feasts, but Israel (old and new) partakes of each one.

Pentecost testifies of Israel's inclusion in a covenant relationship with God. At Pentecost both Jew and Gentile (equally laden with sin) are brought into the finished work and become one perfect offering to the Lord. This feast points to the eternal covenant that we, Christ's body, come to know and experience in Him.

Trumpets, Day of Atonement, and Tabernacles paint a variety of pictures of God's goal in and through Israel.[4] Here we see the culmination or objective of salvation towards which we are being led. This is not a spiritual ladder that we climb. In fact, we all begin having received the finished, perfect work of God in Christ. But God's perfect perspective of what Christ has accomplished works in us and becomes our journey of faith as we grow in the revelation of Christ.

Specifically, Trumpets deals with God's call to the soul, the solemn turning and repentance that puts us in the position to know Him, to allow the cross to do its work in us.

---

[4]   Throughout this book, the name Israel will be used to refer to Christ's corporate body in both old and new covenants, because that is precisely what Israel has always been in the Lord's mind. Exodus 4:22 "Israel is My Son, even My Firstborn."

The Day of Atonement shows us our approach, our access to God. It is a Day that involves drawing near to God but also a great division or judgment that removes all flesh and sin from God's sight and brings Israel into the Holy of Holies. In the new covenant, this comes to be a Day that dawns in our hearts when we heed the call of God's trumpet.

The Lord's ultimate goal is seen in the Feast of Tabernacles which speaks of the ultimate dwelling place of God, a perfect union. God said to Moses, "Make me a tabernacle that I might dwell among them."[5]   This feast paints a picture of our experiential union with God in Christ —"I am in the Father, you are in Me, and I in you."[6]   This is also called the Feast of the Ingathering, and so speaks of the true harvest or ingathering of God where the Lord gathers up the fruit of His Seed, the increase of what He planted.

The last three feasts in the seventh month (the number seven speaking of culmination and rest) represent not dates in time or events in history, but the culmination of salvation, or the goal towards which we are being led. I believe that the four months between Pentecost and the last three feasts (120 days) is similar in some ways to Israel's wilderness experience. This time speaks of a journey where we either decide to follow the Lord toward His purpose, or we wander in the desert of our own imaginations and expectations.   The number 120 appears in various other contexts that perhaps point to an experiential transition from flesh to spirit (putting off the old man, putting on the

---

[5]   Exodus 25:8

[6]   John 14:20

new). In the days of Noah, God said He would tolerate flesh for 120 more years. Moses led Israel until age 120 but could not pass into the land. I'm uncertain about the significance of the number 120, but it seems that these four months represent the journey, the transition, the heart's choice to leave the first behind and walk on towards the purpose of God.

Chapter II
Passover

Key Scriptures: *Exod 12:1-51; Num 9:1-14; Deut 16:1-7; Mark 14:12-26; 1Cor 5:6-8; Heb 11:27-29*

Passover is the first of the spring feasts, and begins on the fourteenth day of the first month. In the mind of an old covenant Jew, these three feasts in the first month were grouped together and often referred to collectively as the Feast of Unleavened Bread. Though Passover is certainly described in Scripture as its own separate feast, the gospels sometimes refer to Passover as "the first day of Unleavened Bread."[7]

The Feast of Passover was a meal eaten on the fourteenth day of the first month (Abib or Nisan) that commemorated the actual Passover *event* of Exodus 12. At the first Passover, Israel was placed by God into the death of the lamb. They were told to slay a perfect lamb, paint its blood over their door posts, *enter* into the house covered with blood, and *eat* the lamb in its entirety. Meanwhile, as

---

[7]   Matthew 26:17

Israel ate their judgment *in* the lamb, Egypt received their judgment *outside of* the lamb.

With Passover God *begins* His purpose with Israel. It is the beginning of His involvement with them, the beginning of their experience of Him, the beginning of the process. In Passover the solitary Seed of God is sown (into death) with great expectation for a harvest.

> **Exod 12:1** Now the LORD spoke to Moses and Aaron in the land of Egypt, saying, 2 "This month shall be your <u>beginning of months</u>; it shall be the first month of the year to you."

This feast was the basis for the covenant, the foundation for the relationship that God established with His people. Without this feast, Israel would remain in their sin, separated from God.

> **Num 9:13** But the man who...ceases to keep the Passover, <u>that same person shall be cut off from among his people</u> because he did not bring the offering of the Lord at its appointed time; <u>that man shall bear his sin</u>.

Not bringing the offering to the Lord at its appointed time was the type and shadow of failing to relate to God in His Son, or failing to know Christ as the Person and Place in Whom one could relate to God. Not offering this offering to the Lord is like trying to establish a relationship with God in Adam, the natural man, the flesh. Such a relationship does not exist.   Without Passover, there is no Israel, because until they are baptized into the lamb, all who live in the land of Egypt are dead in sin and transgression.

It is important to understand that God has no relationship with man outside the boundaries of His Son. As Isaiah says more than once, God has given us His Son *as* our covenant, *as* our relationship with the Father.[8] Many Christians speak as though each believer has their own private relationship with God.   But the truth is far better than this. The truth is that God has granted us access into the one perfect relationship that He has with Jesus Christ. Either we come to share Christ's relationship with His Father, or we do not have the Father or the Son. Therefore, when Israel ate the slain lamb on Passover, they were then and there (in type and shadow) baptized into Christ. They now had a relationship with God that nobody else on earth enjoyed, and therefore no foreigner (no foreign un-circumcised seed) was allowed to eat this feast. A foreigner could be joined to Israel and enjoy this relationship but *only* through circumcision, a picture of the cross, the removal of flesh by the shedding of blood.   Once circumcised, a foreigner could eat the Passover lamb.

> ***Exod 12:43***   *And the LORD said to Moses and Aaron, "This is the ordinance of the Passover: <u>No foreigner shall eat it</u>. 44 But every man's servant who is bought for money, <u>when you have circumcised him, then he may eat it</u>. 45   A sojourner and a hired servant shall not eat it."*

---

[8]   Isaiah 42:6, 49:8

The blood was painted on the door posts only the first year, during the actual Passover event. But Israel had to keep the feast each year by reenacting the remainder of the Exodus 12 symbolism involving the lamb. Every year they killed the lamb at twilight, entered a home with a group large enough to eat one lamb, and ate the entire lamb with unleavened bread and bitter herbs.

Passover as God's Judgment

This feast speaks of the judgment of the world through the death of Christ. In one way or another, all those living in the land of Egypt died on the fourteenth of the first month. Some died in the lamb, others died outside of the lamb, but everyone died. The one death was a death unto resurrection; the other was a death unto destruction.

Shortly before the cross, Jesus said "now is the judgment of the world...and if I am lifted up from the earth, I will draw all men to Myself."[9] Later, describing this same reality, Paul writes, "If One died for all, then all died."[10] Every adamic man and woman was crucified with Christ whether they realize it or not. The judgment of God through the cross was universal. However, the resurrection that follows death is only for those who are born again, those who receive Christ by faith as their resurrection and their life.

---

[9] John 12:31-32
[10] 2 Corinthians 5:14

Therefore, you could say that there are two distinct ways to receive or experience the death of Christ represented by Passover. Those who accept this death as their own judgment, those who agree with it, partake of it, eat it, these are given a new life in the "morning"—the dawning of a new day. When a heart agrees with God's judgment of the sin and death in the adamic man, it is given Christ not only as its death, but also as its resurrection. However, those who refuse this death as their own well-deserved judgment will never escape the adamic man nor the law of sin and death that reigns in that man. These too are judged in the death of the Lamb but, refusing the gift of life in Christ, they remain in Egypt (sin and death), separated from God's covenant.

Participation in the Lamb's Death

In several clear prophetic pictures, we see that Israel had to experience in themselves the death of the lamb. The entire assembly killed their lamb at the same moment signifying one great corporate death. They then painted the blood around their doors, entered into the house and ate the entire lamb. And because they were participating in His death, they could not come out until the morning when they had finished the meal.[11] They could not come out from that house of judgment until Christ began a new day in a brand

---

[11] Exodus 12:6-22

new light. In the morning, Egypt could no longer hold them.

This meal was not supposed to be a celebratory or savory feast. Eating the lamb was a picture of participation in death, not a picture of enjoying God's delicious provision. The meal was not a pleasant experience. They were to eat "its head with its legs and its entrails...with unleavened bread and bitter herbs."[12]

Incidentally, Judas did not finish the Passover meal when he ate together with Christ the night of His betrayal. Unlike the other disciples, he went out "into the night."[13] Perhaps this is why he is called "son of perdition" or "son of destruction." Maybe Judas represents the adamic man that refuses the lamb and bears his own judgment. Judas was offered new life in Christ but refused the purpose for which he was born.

Jesus said, "Woe to that man by whom the Son of Man is betrayed! It would have been good for that man if he had never been born."[14] I believe Jesus was not only speaking of the individual man Judas, but also of what Judas represented. Judas was a man invited to eat the Passover with Christ, to "dip with Him in the dish,"[15] and find life in the light of a new day. But like his father Adam in the garden, Judas refused and betrayed the Life he was offered.

---

[12] Exodus 12:8,9

[13] John 13:30

[14] Matthew 26:24

[15] Mark 14:20

When I See The Blood

God did not pass over the houses of Israel to indicate the Israelites were *escaping* death and judgment, but rather because the blood indicated that they were *already dead and judged* in the lamb. This is extremely important.

Like several other pictures given to us in the Old Testament, what was under the blood represented that which had *already* been judged of God—a condition in which there was now no more condemnation. God related to His people under this covering, as those in whom there was nothing left to judge. We see this same reality shown to us in the rainbow that followed the great flood. In the story of Noah, God's judgment had been perfectly executed in the flood, and afterwards, to those who now lived under covering of the rainbow, He promised never again to destroy the earth. The rainbow was a sign to God that judgment had passed and that He was now at peace with His creation. He said, "When I see the rainbow in the clouds, I will remember my covenant."[16]

In the same way, God sends the Destroyer to Egypt to execute His perfect judgment. But echoing the declaration He made after the flood, God says, "When I see the blood, I will pass over you; and the plague shall not be on you to destroy you."[17] Israel was judged in the lamb, but they were not destroyed. And when God saw the blood painted over their houses, He recognized that the ones dwelling under

---

[16] Genesis 9:16
[17] Exodus 12:13

this covering had already died—there was nothing left to judge.

An Eternal Division

In Exodus, we can see that the death of the lamb, and the subsequent exodus, established a perfect division or separation between Egypt and God (together with His people). A greater view of this division will be discussed in the Feast of Unleavened Bread.

God's judgment did not end the existence of Egypt, but it perfectly ended Israel's relationship to it.

> ***Exod 14:13*** *"Do not be afraid. Stand still, and see the salvation of the LORD, which He will accomplish for you today. For the Egyptians whom you see today, you shall see again no more forever."*

Israel literally never saw Egypt again because God's judgment was perfect and permanent. However, failing to experience this judgment in their hearts, Israel still saw themselves as citizens of Egypt and often longed to go back to the familiar land of sin and death. Nearly the entire first generation lived in the fear of death, in blindness, and an internal slavery to an already defeated enemy.

Nevertheless, from God's perspective they had been crucified to Egypt, and Egypt had been crucified to them.

They had been "translated out of the kingdom of darkness and conveyed into the kingdom of the Son of His Love."[18] Once they entered into the death of Christ (the blood covered door) on that first evening, from God's vantage point they had left Egypt. Naturally speaking, they left the following morning, and crossed the Red Sea three days later. But from God's point of view, Israel was separated from Egypt the very night that they were baptized into the death of the lamb. Notice how the Lord describes this reality when talking to Moses in Deuteronomy 16.

> **Deut 16:1** *"For in the month of Abib the LORD your God brought you out of Egypt by night... 6 but at the place where the LORD your God chooses to make His name abide, there you shall sacrifice the Passover at twilight, at the going down of the sun, at the time you came out of Egypt.*

Thus eating the lamb implied an immediate exodus, and God made sure to illustrate this by having all of Israel eat the lamb dressed for a journey.

> **Exod 12:11** *And thus you shall eat it: with a belt on your waist, your sandals on your feet, and your staff in your hand. So you shall eat it in haste. It is the LORD's Passover.*

---

[18] Colossians 1:13

One of the most important things that we need to understand about Passover is that, from God's perspective, eating His lamb and leaving Egypt were the same reality. Therefore, even as Israel was finishing the meal, Pharaoh (always a picture of Satan, the king of sin, death, and slavery) cried out to Moses, "Rise, go out from among my people, both you and the children of Israel."[19] Now having nothing more to do with that land or its king, it is as though Israel was projected or vomited out of Egypt.

The Fulfillment of Passover

Every aspect of the Passover event and the yearly commemorative feast finds its fulfillment in the person and work of Christ.   The fulfillment of Passover is both an objective work accomplished by Christ through bearing the death and judgment of the adamic man, as well as an inward experience in every believer as we "keep the feast" and subjectively experience all that this death implies.

Many Christians do not realize that Jesus was literally crucified on the actual day of Passover after eating the Passover lamb with His disciples. The Jewish day always began in the evening at the setting of the sun and ended the following evening at the same time.   So Christ ate the Passover meal with His disciples after sunset when Passover was just beginning. He was betrayed and arrested that night, tried before Pontius Pilate in the morning, and

---

[19]   Exodus 12:31

crucified in the afternoon. All of this took place on the day of Passover, the fourteenth of the first month.

> **Matt 26:2** *You know that after two days is the Passover, and the Son of Man will be delivered up to be crucified.*

We have already discussed how, as this day was approaching, Jesus declared His cross to be the judgment of the adamic man, saying, "Now is the judgment of the world."[20]   But just like we saw with Israel and Egypt, to some this judgment would be death unto life, but to others it would be death unto destruction.   I believe with this reality in mind, Jesus said:

> **Matt 21:44**   *And whoever falls on this stone will be broken; but on whomever it falls, it will grind him to powder."*

John the Baptist spoke of these same two options. The one receiving Christ passes from death to life, but the one not believing remains in Egypt under the wrath of God.

> **John 3:36** *He who believes in the Son has everlasting life; and he who does not believe the Son shall not see life, but the wrath of God abides on him.*

---

[20]   John 12:31

Jesus was very clear that His death on Passover was the fulfillment of the feast, and the beginning of the true and eternal covenant with God.

> **Mark 14:22** *And as they were eating [the Passover], Jesus took bread, blessed and broke it, and gave it to them and said, "Take, eat; this is My body." 23 Then He took the cup, and when He had given thanks He gave it to them, and they all drank from it. 24 And He said to them, "This is My blood of the new covenant, which is shed for many."*

Even before the night of Passover, Jesus had taught plainly that eating the lamb (eating His flesh and drinking His blood) was the only way to make the exodus from death unto life.

> **John 6:53** *Most assuredly, I say to you, unless you eat the flesh of the Son of Man and drink His blood, you have no life in you... 55 For My flesh is true food , and My blood is true drink. 56 He who eats My flesh and drinks My blood abides in Me, and I in him.*

And so with the fulfillment of Passover, God begins His true and eternal purpose with Spiritual Israel. The cross is the beginning of His involvement with them and their experience of Him. Through the cross, God planted His one perfect Seed into the earth with great expectation for a multi-membered, resurrected harvest. With this in mind, consider some of the following verses.

> **John 12:24** *Most assuredly, I say to you, unless a grain of wheat falls into the ground and dies, it remains alone; but if it dies, it produces much grain.*

> **Matt 13:3** *Behold, a sower went out to sow... But others fell on good ground and yielded a crop: some a hundredfold, some sixty, some thirty.*

> **Rom 7:4** *Therefore, my brethren, you also have become dead to the law through the body of Christ, that you may be joined to another—to Him who was raised from the dead, that we should bear fruit to God.*

Lastly, through the cross of Christ, God fulfilled the great division or separation that we saw take place in Exodus 12-14. He established an eternal boundary between the first and second, Egypt and Israel, Adam and Christ, death and life, etc. For those who eat the Lamb, we are literally translated out of one realm and man, and into Another.

> **Col 1:13** *He has delivered us from the power of darkness and translated us into the kingdom of the Son of His love.*

Eph 2:5 *Even when we were dead in trespasses, made us alive together with Christ (by grace you have been saved) 6 and raised us up together, and made us sit together in the heavenly places in Christ Jesus.*

Gal 6:14 *But God forbid that I should boast except in the cross of our Lord Jesus Christ, by whom the world has been crucified to me, and I to the world.*

Chapter III
The Feast of Unleavened Bread

Key Scriptures: Exod 12:15-20, 12:39, 13:3-10, 23:15, 34:18; Lev 23:6; Num 28:17-25; Deut 16:3-4, 16:8; Mark 14:12; 1 Cor 5:6-8

Unleavened Bread was a seven day ceremony immediately following Passover (starting the fifteenth of Abib/Nisan) in which special sacrifices were made unto God, no work was done (on the first and last day of the feast), and most notably, all leaven was completely removed from both the bread and the houses in Israel. In almost every occurrence in the Bible,[21] leaven is a picture of the nature of sin that lives, grows, ferments, and corrupts.

With Unleavened Bread, the second day of the first three feast days, God puts away *sin* (not just *sins*), buries it in the earth, and leaves it there forever. This feast speaks of the perfect and permanent separation brought about through the death of the Lamb—the total removal of God's

---

[21] With the probable exception of Matthew 13:33/Luke 13:21 where the kingdom of God is compared to leaven in its ability to grow and fill three measures of meal.

loaf from the fallenness, corruption, and death of the first. In this feast we see a loaf of bread that represents a new state of existence.

Separation/Division is the Key Aspect

We spoke of the great division in our treatment of Passover because the two feasts are so intricately tied together. We will deal with it in more detail here. When God describes the *reason* that Israel must keep this feast, He connects Unleavened Bread to their total separation and exodus from the dead and corrupt house of Egypt. Notice this connection in the following verses.

> **Exod 12:17** *So you shall observe the Feast of Unleavened Bread, for on this same day I will have brought your armies out of the land of Egypt.*

> **Exod 13:7** *Unleavened bread shall be eaten seven days. And no leavened bread shall be seen among you, nor shall leaven be seen among you in all your quarters. 8 And you shall tell your son in that day, saying, 'This is done because of what the LORD did for me when I came up from Egypt.' 9 It shall be as a sign to you on your hand and as a memorial between your eyes, that the LORD's law may be in your mouth; for with a strong hand the LORD has brought you out of Egypt.*

Each of these spring feasts are first realities that Christ experienced alone, and then they become the experience of every believer who comes to live in Him. Christ passed through death, burial, and resurrection as the only Seed of His kind. But by receiving Christ by faith, His death becomes our judgment, His burial our transformation, and His resurrection the life that we know as our own.

As I have mentioned, I believe that these first three feasts correspond to the death, burial, and resurrection of Christ. This second feast relates to the reality of burial. Jesus remained buried during the entire first day of Unleavened Bread, the fifteenth of Nisan, and then rose on the feast of Firstfruits, the third day.

Burial is what we do when someone has died and the time has come to put them out of our sight forever. By burying someone, we end our relationship with that person and give them back to the earth from which they came —"For dust you are, and to dust you will return."[22] When we leave someone in the grave, we understand that it is time to move on without them, to relate with them no longer. When Sarah died, Abraham said, "Give me property for a burial place, that I may bury my dead out of my sight."[23] This is precisely what Christ's death accomplished with relation to sin. Christ gathered up into Himself all of Adam, not just his sins but the nature of sin itself. He bore the judgment of that man and brought him into an eternal condition of separation from God. Then, having finished His work, He arose on the third day leaving Adam behind in

---

[22] Genesis 3:19
[23] Genesis 23:4

the earth and divided from God forever. This is very much like what happens when a seed dies and falls into the earth. Though the life within the seed rises again and bears fruit, the husk dies and remains part of the earth forever.

I believe this is exactly what God is showing us in the Feast of Unleavened bread.   Through the death of the Passover lamb, God judges all who are in Egypt and then brings out "Israel My Son, even My Firstborn."[24]   When Israel walks out in the morning, God separates His new loaf from the leaven that once filled and defined them. For us who have found in Christ the fulfillment of this feast, this means separating the soul from sin, from the adamic nature. We become "dead to sin, and alive to God in Christ Jesus."[25]

Once again, this separation (or sanctification) was first Christ's experience in leaving Adam in the grave, rising from the dead, and returning to His Father. But as with all of the feasts, Christ's experience of the cross becomes a progressive realization for all who are born of His Spirit. For this reason Jesus said:

> **John 17:16** *They are not of the world, just as I am not of the world... 19 And for their sakes I sanctify Myself, that they also may be sanctified by the truth.*

> **John 14:19**   *A little while longer and the world will see Me no more, but you will see Me. Because I*

---

[24]   Exodus 4:22
[25]   Romans 6:11

*live, you will live also. 20 At that day you will
know that I am in My Father, and you in Me, and I
in you.*

A New Loaf

As we saw in the previous section, partaking of the lamb
was the cause of Israel's expulsion out of the land of sin,
death, and slavery. They ate the lamb with the immediate
expectation of leaving.   But this leaving, from God's
perspective, involved much more than leaving a *place*. It
involved leaving a condition or state of being as well. Thus
the story of Israel's physical exodus from Egypt is given to
us together with another important picture—a changed or
transformed loaf. Israel was now a new creation, a new
loaf, one that has been set free from the leaven that filled
and governed every aspect of their being.

In the Bible, the first three feasts are often collectively
called by the name Unleavened Bread. Perhaps the reason
for this is that this dramatic transformation (first
experienced by Christ—from Last Adam to Second Man[26]—
and then experienced by us in Christ) is the center and
focus of the spring feasts.

As strange as it may sound, on the morning of the
fifteenth of Nisan (the first day of Unleavened Bread) Israel
began their march out of Egypt carrying unleavened loaves
in their hands, and kneading bowls (vessels for the bread)
on their shoulders and bound up in their clothes.

---

[26]   1 Corinthians 15:45

Exod 12:33 *And the Egyptians urged the people, that they might send them out of the land in haste. For they said, "We shall all be dead." 34* <u>*So the people took their dough before it was leavened, having their kneading bowls bound up in their clothes on their shoulders*</u>.

It seems almost silly to imagine two or three million people marching out of Egypt carrying bread and bowls, but the Lord was carefully painting a natural picture of a spiritual reality to come. Again, leaving Egypt was not just the exodus from a difficult situation; it was a trans-formation of nature (unleavened loaves) that made us fit vessels (bowls) for the glory of the Lord. A similar picture is given to us by Isaiah the prophet when he describes Israel's future exodus from captivity in Babylon.

Isa 52:11 *Depart! Depart! Go out from there, Touch no unclean thing; Go out from the midst of her, Be clean,* <u>*You who bear the vessels of the LORD*</u>.

The Plundering of Egypt

In the midst of this great separation and exodus there is another view of our salvation that emerges. Not only are we shown to be a new unleavened loaf carrying the vessels of the Lord, but our exodus is also the means by which God plunders the enemy's camp.

> **Exod 12:35** *Now the children of Israel had done according to the word of Moses, and they had asked from the Egyptians <u>articles of silver, articles of gold, and clothing</u>. 36 And the LORD had given the people favor in the sight of the Egyptians, so that they granted them what they requested. <u>Thus they plundered the Egyptians.</u>*

These articles of silver, gold, and cloth were not taken to make the individual Israelites rich. Rather, they were used of the Lord (later in Exodus) to build the Tabernacle of God, His dwelling place among the people. I believe the picture we are meant to see here is that God not only defeated His enemy, but also took or plundered the spoils of war (our souls!) with which He then built His own house. The Lord robbed from Satan's camp the precious materials, vessels, articles (again, redeemed souls) that are then transformed into His literal dwelling place, the temple where He is glorified.

Knowing what God has Done

As with all other realities of salvation, there is always the objective finished work of God in Christ *and* there is our subjective spiritual comprehension (faith) and experience of this finished work. So being an unleavened loaf and knowing this reality are not the same. In other words, *being* dead to sin and separated from Adam, does not necessarily mean that you are *experiencing* this great transformation.

A clear picture of this can be seen in the exodus story. Old covenant Israel became dead to Egypt just as soon as they entered the blood covered door. But it was not until forty years later, when by faith they crossed the Jordan, that they began to *experience* their freedom from Egypt, the land that God had long ago put away. Notice what the Lord says on the day that Joshua led them across the Jordan.

> **Josh 5:9** *Then the LORD said to Joshua, "<u>This day</u> I have rolled away the reproach of Egypt from you."*

In the first century, new covenant Israel (the spiritual body of Christ) had the exact same problem. They *were* a new creation, but many were not experiencing the greatness of their transformation because their hearts were not turning to the Lord. They had received salvation, but they did not know the salvation that they had received. Through new birth they had been given the life of Christ, but they were not coming to know Christ by the revelation of the Spirit of Truth. Paul dealt with this issue often in the church, and in one instance he used the language of this feast to do so.

> **1Cor 5:6** *Your glorying is not good. Do you not know that a little leaven leavens the whole lump? 7*

Therefore purge out the old leaven, that you may be a new lump, <u>since you truly are unleavened</u>. For indeed Christ, our Passover, was sacrificed for us. 8 Therefore let us keep the feast, not with old leaven, nor with the leaven of malice and wickedness, but with the unleavened bread of purity and truth.

Notice how Paul understood this feast and how he applied it to the church's condition in Corinth. Christ the Passover Lamb had been sacrificed. It therefore follows that these believers "truly are unleavened," regardless of whether or not they were "keeping the feast;" that is, knowing and walking in the reality of this division between old and new. So Paul admonishes them to "keep the feast" as a way of saying, "Now you must come to know and live the truth."

Keeping the Feast

As with all seven of the feasts, the act of keeping the feast represented personal acceptance, participation, and obedience (alignment) with what God was declaring through the ceremony. As we mentioned briefly, under the old covenant, the Feast of Unleavened Bread was a seven day ceremony that involved three primary elements: 1) special sacrifices were to be offered, all representing some aspect of Christ's work, 2) no work was to be done on the first and last day of the feast, 3) and the most notable requirement was the total prohibition of any trace of leaven, both in their meals and in their homes.

> **Exod 12:14** *So this day shall be to you a memorial; and you shall keep it as a feast to the LORD throughout your generations. You shall keep it as a feast by an everlasting ordinance. 15 Seven days you shall eat unleavened bread. On the first day you shall remove leaven from your houses. <u>For whoever eats leavened bread from the first day until the seventh day, that person shall be cut off from Israel</u>.*

> **Exod 13:7** *Unleavened bread shall be eaten seven days. And no leavened bread shall be seen among you, <u>nor shall leaven be seen among you in all your dwellings</u>.*

> **Deut 16:4** *And no leaven shall be seen among you <u>in all your territory</u> for seven days.*

Keeping the feast under the old covenant meant physically walking out this *testimony* of a new creation. For seven days this feast painted a picture of a people free from sin, delivered from the nature of Adam. Israel had to outwardly align with the perspective of God in this figurative, symbolic way at an appointed time and for a specific purpose.

Under the New Covenant, Paul shows us that "keeping the feast" is no longer a natural ceremony, but rather a spiritual reality that involves knowing and experiencing this perfect separation. We are no longer acting out the shadow of things to come, but we are learning (by the Spirit) the reality of what has come and thereby being inwardly cleansed from every residue of the adamic man that clings to our unrenewed minds. In this way we "purge out the old leaven," and "keep the feast... with the unleavened bread of purity and truth."[27]   Paul understood that the work was finished, and that we, having been placed by God in Christ, are a new creation in Him.

> **2 Cor 5:17** *Therefore, if anyone is in Christ, <u>he is a new creation; old things have passed away; behold, all things have become new</u>.*

> **Rom 6:4** *Therefore we were buried with Him through baptism into death, that just as Christ was raised from the dead by the glory of the Father, even so we also should walk in <u>newness of life</u>...* 6 Knowing this, <u>that our old man was crucified with Him, that the body of sin might be done away with</u>, that we should no longer be slaves of sin. 7 <u>For he who has died has been freed from sin</u>.

Having been baptized into a finished work, our responsibility and our calling is to keep the feast, aligning our souls with the finished work of the cross. This is not a single decision that we make, but rather a daily process that

---

[27]   1 Corinthians 5:6-8

the Bible calls "the renewing of the spirit of the mind."[28] By nature our mind is hostile towards God, and perfectly ignorant of His life and His way. This does not immediately change when we are born again. New birth is when we receive the life of Christ, but the light of His life must shine in our hearts to progressively cause our hearts to walk in His perspective, His truth. We never need more of His life, but we need to learn to walk in the light as He is in the light and experience His fellowship with the Father.[29] This is what Paul calls coming to "know even as we are known"[30] or "apprehending that for which we have been apprehended by God."[31]

None Shall Appear Before Me Empty-Handed

God's view of "keeping the feasts" (in both covenants) has to do with presenting back to Him some aspect of Christ that has first been given to Israel by God. This was God's expectation in each of the seven feasts—to see Israel appear before Him and relate to Him in Christ.

Exod 23:15 You shall keep the Feast of Unleavened Bread. You shall eat unleavened bread seven days, as I commanded you, at the time appointed

---

[28]   Ephesians 4:23
[29]   1 John 1:7
[30]   1 Corinthians 13:12
[31]   Philippians 3:12

in the month of Abib, for in it you came out of Egypt; <u>none shall appear before Me empty.</u>

Appearing before the Lord "empty" would be appearing before Him in the nakedness and emptiness of the adamic man with nothing of Christ to present to the Father. This is what Paul would call "nullifying the grace of God,"[32] that is, refusing to walk in, live by, and present to the Father all that has been given to us in Christ.

We need to understand that grace gives to us all that God requires in and as the person of Christ, but it also *requires* back what God has given. Many types and shadows and parables demonstrate that God gives us all that we need and all that He wants, but they also demonstrate that the increase of what He has given us is God's only expectation.

> *__Matt 25:26__ But his lord answered and said to him, 'You wicked and lazy servant, you knew that I reap where I have not sown, and gather where I have not scattered seed. 27 So you ought to have deposited my money with the bankers, and at my coming I would have <u>received back my own</u> with interest.*

> *__Matt 13:23__ But he who received seed on the good ground is he who hears the word and understands it, who indeed bears fruit and produces: some a hundredfold, some sixty, some thirty.*

---

[32]   Galatians 2:21

There are many erroneous views of grace in the Lord's body. Often we speak of grace as though it were merely the forgiveness of Adam's shortcomings. The gift of forgiveness is certainly included in grace, but grace is far greater than forgiveness. Grace is a relationship where God gives to us, and works in us, everything that He wants from us. He gave us a death that we could not die, and a life that we could not live. By grace, Christ is made unto us all things— wisdom, righteousness, redemption, life, light, glory, etc. But again, what we often fail to realize that having given us all that Christ is by grace, God then requires and desires from us only that which is the work of His grace. For this reason, Paul says things like this:

> **1 Cor 15:10** *But by the grace of God I am what I am, and His grace toward me was not in vain; but I labored more abundantly than they all, yet not I, but the grace of God which was with me.*

> **Heb 12:28** *Therefore, since we are receiving a kingdom which cannot be shaken, let us have grace, by which we may serve God acceptably with reverence and godly fear. For our God is a consuming fire.*

Chapter IV
The Feast of Firstfruits

Key Scriptures: *Exod 23:19, 34:26; Lev 23:9-14; Deut 26:1-10; Jer 2:3; Matt 28:1; Mark 16:1; Luke 24:1; 1 Cor 15:20*

Firstfruits was the third of the first three feasts, and fell on the day *after* the first Sabbath *after* the fifteenth of the month (the beginning of Unleavened Bread). Whenever the fifteenth of the month fell on a Sabbath, the first three feasts would fall on consecutive days. This was the case the year that Christ was crucified. He was crucified on the fourteenth, remained buried during the fifteenth (a Sabbath), rose from the dead on Firstfruits, the sixteenth of the month.

During the Feast of Firstfruits, Israel had to bring a single sheaf of the firstfruits of the harvest of the land to the priest. The priest would wave the sheaf before the Lord, and it would be accepted on behalf of Israel. Along with the sheaf, a male lamb without blemish was offered to the Lord as a burnt offering.

> **Lev 23:9** *And the LORD spoke to Moses, saying,*
> *10 "Speak to the children of Israel, and say to*
> *them: 'When you come into the land which I give to*
> *you, and reap its harvest, then you shall bring a*
> *sheaf of the firstfruits of your harvest to the priest.*
> *11 He shall wave the sheaf before the LORD, to be*
> *accepted on your behalf; on the day after the*
> *Sabbath the priest shall wave it.'"*

As we have already noted, this feast speaks of Christ's resurrection and the presentation of Himself before the Father as the "firstborn from among the dead."[33]   Christ is the acceptable offering through whom and in whom all of Israel is accepted into God's presence.

The Head of a New Humanity

In His resurrection, Christ opened the womb of death and became the firstborn of a new kind, or race, that are joined to Him by faith. This is not to say that there are many others like Christ, but that, through His resurrection, Christ has become the source and life of His body the church. As such He is said to be the Head of a new man, the initiation of a new creation.

---

[33]   Colossians 1:18

Rom 8:29 *For whom He foreknew, He also predestined to be conformed to the image of His Son, <u>that He might be the firstborn among many brethren</u>.*

Col 1:18 *And He is the head of the body, the church, who is the beginning, the <u>firstborn from the dead</u>, that in all things He may have the preeminence.*

God now knows and relates to all human beings in one of two men—Adam or Christ. In Adam, man is dead in sin and transgression, still a slave in Egypt to a cruel and exacting king. But in Christ, we are made alive, raised up, and seated with Christ in heavenly places. We are "heirs of God and joint heirs with Christ."[34]

The Acceptable Offering

Just as the first sheaf of the barley crop came out of the soil, was waved by the priest before the Lord, and was accepted on behalf of the people, so too Christ, the firstborn from among the dead, is presented before God as the acceptable offering. He is the One *in whom and because of whom* the body of Christ is accepted.

Heb 9:24 *For Christ has not entered the holy places made with hands, which are copies of the*

---

[34] Romans 8:17

*true, but into heaven itself, <u>now to appear in the</u>
<u>presence of God for us</u>.*

It is important to realize that this appearing in the
presence of God "for us," does not mean *instead of* us. The
Greek word here is *huper,* and means *"on behalf of, for the
sake of."* The difference is important because, as His body,
we were raised up into the presence of God with Him.
Obviously our bodies remain on earth, but as far as our
souls are concerned, "we have died and our life is hidden
with Christ in God."[35] With this reality in mind, Paul says,
"If then you were raised with Christ, seek those things
which are above."[36] So we are there with Christ, but He is
the one appearing. We have been brought into the presence
of God, but Christ is the one seen, recognized, and received
on behalf of us. In the resurrection, Christ has presented
Himself as the acceptable firstfruits offering and it is *in
Him* that we are accepted.

Eph 1:6 *To the praise of the glory of His grace, by
which <u>He made us accepted in the Beloved</u>.*

The First to Return to the Father's House

As the firstfruits, and the firstborn from the dead, Christ
was the first to return to the Father's house.

---

[35] Colossians 3:3
[36] Colossians 3:1

Exod 23:19 *The first of the firstfruits of your land* <u>*you shall bring into the house of the LORD your*</u> <u>*God*</u>.

Deut 26:1 *And it shall be, when you come into the land which the LORD your God is giving you as an inheritance, and you possess it and dwell in it, 2 that you shall take some of* <u>*the first of all the*</u> <u>*produce of the ground*</u>, *which you shall bring from your land that the LORD your God is giving you, and put it in a basket and* <u>*go to the place where the*</u> <u>*LORD your God chooses to make His name abide.*</u>

Before returning to His Father, Christ first prepared a place for us through the work of His cross. Through His death, burial, and resurrection, Christ did exactly what He promised to the disciples: He opened the heavens[37] and made a way for us to be with Him where He is. This reality is precisely what Christ was trying to explain to His disciples in the days immediately preceding His cross. He had to die, be buried, and rise again in order to open the way to the Father's house, "lead captivity captive." and bring them there with Him.

John 14:1 *Let not your heart be troubled; you believe in God, believe also in Me. 2 In My Father's house are many mansions; if it were not so, I*

---

[37]   John 1:51

would have told you. I go to prepare a place for you.

John 17:24 *Father, I desire that they also whom You gave Me may be with Me where I am, that they may behold My glory which You have given Me; for You loved Me before the foundation of the world.*

This is *not* a future reality that Christians should be waiting for. This is the present and eternal reality of every believing soul that has been baptized into Christ's death, and raised with Him in newness of life. Sadly, so many Christians believe that the death of the *physical body* is the great transition, or exodus, for the human soul. The Bible does not agree with this idea. Throughout the New Testament, the apostles are unanimous and emphatic that experiencing the death *of the cross* is how we pass from one man and creation to another. Again, the natural vessel does not change location. It does not need to. Through the cross the human soul is literally translated out of one realm and man and into Another.

The Believer's Experience of Firstfruits

As with the other feasts, the Feast of Firstfruits is first an accomplishment and experience of Christ alone. But through our participation in Christ by faith, it also becomes the journey of each believer. We are joined by faith to

Christ's finished work.   Therefore this resurrection from among the dead, this coming out of the earth like the stem of a plant shooting out of the ground, *and* this returning to the Father's house becomes our reality and experience as well.   The Spirit-given discovery of this reality is the foundation of our journey of faith. Paul says:

> **Eph 2:5** *Even when we were dead in trespasses, made us alive together with Christ (by grace you have been saved), 6 and raised us up together, and made us sit together in the heavenly places in Christ Jesus.*

This was not a matter of theology for Paul. Nor was it a mere *positional* truth that awaited a future consummation.   This was Paul's reality, and it was what he knew to be the reality of every man and woman in Christ. Too often we study verses like these as theological concepts instead of waking up to the realities being described by them.   To the church in Ephesus Paul says, "Wake up O sleeper, rise from among the dead, and Christ will give you light."[38]

Receiving Christ by faith means we are placed into Him, and that His journey through death, burial, and resurrection becomes ours as well.

> **Rom 6:3** *Or do you not know that as many of us as were baptized into Christ Jesus were baptized into His death? 4 Therefore we were buried with*

---
[38] Ephesians 5:14

Him through baptism into death, that just as Christ was raised from the dead by the glory of the Father, even so we also should walk in newness of life. 5 For if we have been united [Lit. <u>planted together</u>] in the likeness of His death, certainly we also shall be in the likeness of His resurrection.

In these verses, Paul describes our union with Christ as being *planted together* like a seed into death. Those who are planted with Christ in death, come out of the ground with Christ in resurrection. This is the believer's experience of Firstfruits. The firstfruits of the barley crop rose out from the dead earth and was brought into the temple of the Lord. In like manner, the soul of every believer leaves the earth with Him and finds its new home in the Father's house.

The Manifestation of Firstfruits

Once again, Christ was crucified on Passover, remained buried during the Feast of Unleavened Bread (a Sabbath), and then rose from among the dead and left the tomb on the third day, the day of the Feast of Firstfruits.

Matt 28:1 <u>Now after the Sabbath, as the first day of the week began to dawn</u>, Mary Magdalene and the other Mary came to see the tomb.

Luke 24:1 <u>*Now on the first day of the week, very*</u> <u>*early in the morning,*</u> *they, and certain other women with them, came to the tomb bringing the spices which they had prepared.*

The Feast of Firstfruits did not always fall on the third day after Passover. It fell on the day after the Sabbath after Passover. So, for instance, if Passover fell on a Tuesday one year, Unleavened Bread would begin on Wednesday, and Firstfruits would still be the day after the next Sabbath. So, in this case, there would be six days between Passover and Firstfruits. However, clearly by divine orchestration, the year Christ was crucified Passover fell on a Friday, Unleavened Bread was on the Sabbath, and therefore Firstfruits fell on the third day, the day Christ said He would rise again.

A Note of Clarification

One thing that can be confusing about the feasts is that they are often called by more than one name in the Bible. Some of them have as many as three or four different names. Perhaps the most confusing issue that arises with this is that, at times, both the third and the fourth feasts (Firstfruits and Pentecost) are called The Feast of Firstfruits.

The reason for this is as follows: As we have mentioned, the cycle of the seven feasts is tied to the planting and harvest season in Israel. However, there was more than one

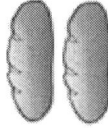

First Three Feasts

Christ's Work Alone

Firstborn From Among The Dead

Barley Harvest

"New Grain" Offering

The Firstfruits of God's Increase Jeremiah 2:3

Last Four Feasts

Our Inclusion In Christ's Work For His Increase / Glory

Wheat

Grapes

Olives

Pomegranates

Figs

crop harvested each year in Israel. First there was the barley harvest (representing Christ's work in the first three feasts). Following barley, there began the far greater portion of Israel's harvest, starting with the wheat that was harvested at Pentecost. I have attempted to illustrate this on the previous page.

Therefore, I believe the reason that both the third and the fourth feast are at times both called Firstfruits is because the one speaks of Christ, the firstborn from among the dead and corresponds to the firstfruits of barley. The other speaks of the church, which is the firstfruits of Christ's increase and corresponds to the firstfruits of wheat.

It was Christ alone in His death, burial, and resurrection that accomplished the judgment, separated the leaven from the loaf, and was raised to His finished work before the Father. This is the firstfruits of barley, and the following verses speak of this reality.

Rom 8:29 For whom He foreknew, He also predestined to be conformed to the image of His Son, that He might be the firstborn among many brethren.

Col 1:18 And He is the head of the body, the church, who is the beginning, the firstborn from the dead, that in all things He may have the preeminence.

1 Cor 15:23 *But each one in his own order: <u>Christ the firstfruits</u>, afterward those who are Christ's at His coming [Lit. in His presence].*

The church as a "new grain offering"[39] is then joined to this perfect work, and the increase of Christ in us becomes the firstfruits of His increase. Notice in the following verses how Israel's beginning (in both the Old and New Testament) is shown to be the firstfruits of Christ's increase in a people.

Jer 2:2 *Go and cry in the hearing of Jerusalem, saying, 'Thus says the LORD: "I remember you, The kindness of your youth, The love of your betrothal, When you went after Me in the wilderness, In a land not sown. 3 Israel was holiness to the LORD, <u>The firstfruits of His increase</u>."*

Jam 1:18 *Of His own will He brought us forth by the word of truth, that <u>we might be a kind of firstfruits of His creatures</u>.*

---

[39] Leviticus 23:16

Chapter V
Pentecost (The Feast of Weeks)

Key Scriptures: *Exod 19:9-25, 23:15-16, 24:1-18, 34:22; Lev 23:15-21; Num 28:26-31; Deut 16:9-12; Acts 2:1-4*

The Feast of Pentecost is the fourth yearly feast of Israel. It took place in the beginning of the third month, exactly fifty days after the firstfruits of barley were waved before the Lord.

Lev 23:15 And you shall count for yourselves from the day after the Sabbath, from the day that you brought the sheaf of the wave offering: seven Sabbaths shall be completed. 16 Count fifty days to the day after the seventh Sabbath; then you shall offer a new grain offering to the LORD.

The name Feast of Weeks comes from the counting of the seven weeks after the Feast of Firstfruits. I am uncertain about the significance of the fifty days. Is this number significant because of the seven sevens? Or should we see here forty days plus ten, since this is how the numbers are mentioned after the resurrection of Christ? Christ appeared to the disciples for *forty* days after His resurrection (Firstfruits), "speaking of the things pertaining to the kingdom of God."[40]   He then told them to wait in Jerusalem for what turned out to be *ten more days* for the gift of the Holy Spirit which came on the Feast of Pentecost.

During the Feast of Pentecost, Israel was required to bring two *leavened* new grain loaves of bread made from wheat, and wave them before the Lord. These two leavened loaves were then offered to the Lord together with a variety of burnt, sin, and peace offerings, and then waved before the Lord together with two lambs.

> **Lev 23:17** *You shall bring from your dwellings two wave loaves of two-tenths of an ephah. They shall be of fine flour; <u>they shall be baked with leaven</u>. <u>They are the firstfruits to the LORD</u>. 18 And you shall offer with the bread seven lambs of the first year, without blemish, one young bull, and two rams. They shall be as a burnt offering to the LORD, with their grain offering and their drink offerings, an offering made by fire for a sweet aroma to the LORD. 19 Then you shall sacrifice one kid of the goats as a sin offering, and two male lambs of the first year as a sacrifice of a peace offering. 20 The priest shall wave them with the*

---

[40]   Acts 1:3

bread of the firstfruits as a wave offering before the LORD, with the two lambs. They shall be holy to the LORD for the priest.

This feast, and the events surrounding it in Exodus 19 and 24, speak in a variety of ways of the church's baptism or inclusion in the finished work of Christ. In the book of Exodus, fifty days after the Feast of Firstfruits, God entered into covenant with Israel, and Israel then entered into the Mountain of God.

The Timing of the Feast

Jewish tradition, along with most Bible commentaries, assert that the timing of this feast corresponds to the inauguration of the Old Testament church. It commemorates the giving of the Law through Moses at Mt. Sinai, and the covenant relationship with God that Israel entered into at Mt. Sinai fifty days after leaving Egypt.

Exod 19:1 In the third month after the going forth of the sons of Israel from the land of Egypt, <u>on this day</u> they entered the wilderness of Sinai.

Israel left Egypt on the fifteenth of the first month. Forty-five days later they arrived at Mt. Sinai. Moses went up the mountain alone for one day; then there were three days of preparation for the entire camp. After these three days, the covenant was established in blood, and the people went up the mountain and met with God. Fifty days in all.[41]

The fifty days here corresponds exactly with the time between Christ's resurrection and the church's reception of the promised Holy Spirit.

The Events Surrounding the First Pentecost

Pentecost (usually called the Feast of Weeks in the Old Testament) was not celebrated until Israel entered the land and sowed and reaped their harvest. But the events that took place at Mt. Sinai, around fifty days after leaving Egypt, are tied to this feast, and clearly point to their new covenant fulfillment.

When they arrived at Sinai, Moses went up the mountain alone and received the instruction from the Lord to put boundary markers around the mountain so that no flesh could come near, touch, or see the Lord who was descending on the mountain in a cloud. The Lord is emphatic about this, demanding that Moses descend the mountain on two separate occasions to warn the Israelites that they cannot approach Him.

> ***Exod 19:12*** *You shall set bounds for the people all around, saying, 'Take heed to yourselves that you do not go up to the mountain or touch its base.*

---

[41] The exact timing of these events is debated by some authors, as well as the meaning of the phrase "on this day" in Exodus 19:1, but I think the big picture of what God is demonstrating is clear nonetheless.

Whoever touches the mountain shall surely be put to death. 13 Not a hand shall touch him, but he shall surely be stoned or shot with an arrow; whether man or beast, he shall not live.' When the trumpet sounds long, they shall come near the mountain.

The picture that we need to understand here is that, until Israel entered into their covenant, they did not have access to God. Until they were born of Spirit (in type and shadow) and joined to God by the blood of the covenant, they were not able to approach Him. His mountain (dwelling place) was entirely off-limits to the flesh.

Moses then announces to the people a *three day* period of purification, sanctification, and washing of clothes, in preparation for meeting with God on the mountain.

Throughout the Old Testament, a three day time period is always a picture of the work of the cross, or of the believer's experience of that work. There are more examples than we could list here, but to name a few: Abraham's three day journey to sacrifice Isaac, the three-day distance that Jacob put between he and Laban, the three days involved in the dreams of the baker and cup-bearer, God's description of Israel's exodus as a three day journey, the three day preparation to cross the Jordan River, David bringing a judgment on all of Israel for three days, Esther asking all Israel to fast for three days before entering the presence of the king, Jonah's three days in the belly of the whale, etc. There are many more.

What God had already completed in the first three feast days (Passover, Unleavened Bread, Firstfruits), is what Israel is now entering into at Pentecost. Their three day participation in the cross of Christ prepares them for what immediately follows—a covenant with God in blood and an approach into His Holy Mountain.

The next four chapters (Exodus 20-23) describe many of the specific laws that Moses received when he was on the mountain alone with God during this time. But when the three day period of sanctification was over, God made His covenant with Israel in blood and invited them into His mountain to see, eat, and drink with Him. The description of these events in Exodus 24 is overflowing with types and shadows that point to the new covenant fulfillment.

First God had Moses write down all of the words of the covenant. He then had Moses build an altar at the base of the mountain along with twelve pillars that represented the twelve tribes of Israel. Moses commanded several young men to offer burnt offerings and peace offerings to the Lord, and they collected the blood of the animals in basins. Half of the blood was sprinkled on the altar, the words of the covenant were read out loud to the people, and then the remainder of the blood was sprinkled on the people while saying, "This is the blood of the covenant which the Lord has made with you according to all these words."[42]

Once the blood had been sprinkled, Moses, Aaron, Nadab and Abihu (Aaron's sons), and seventy elders of Israel (representing the entire congregation) went up the mountain and saw the God of Israel.

---

[42] Exodus 24:8

Exod 24:9 *Then Moses went up, also Aaron, Nadab, and Abihu, and seventy of the elders of Israel, 10 and they saw the God of Israel. And there was under His feet as it were a paved work of sapphire stone, and it was like the very heavens in its clarity. 11 But on the nobles of the children of Israel He did not lay His hand. <u>So they saw God, and they ate and drank.</u>*

While some of the details of this story can be confusing, the general idea seems relatively clear. Roughly fifty days after the first three feasts, God entered into a covenant with the corporate congregation of Israel through blood and invited them all (through Moses, the intercessor) to ascend His mountain and fellowship with Him.

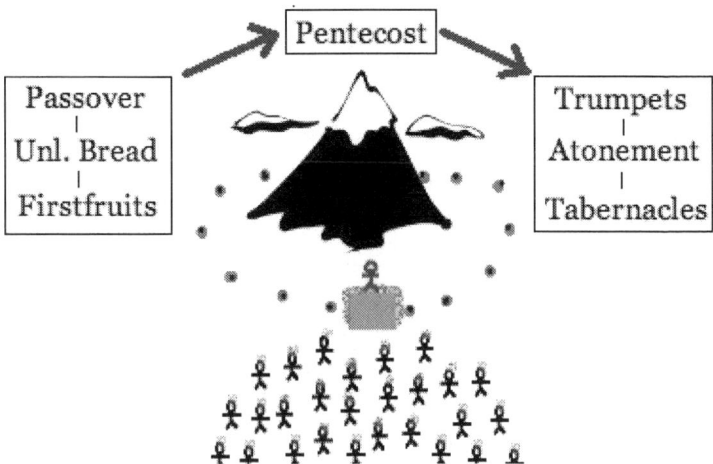

Passover
|
Unl. Bread
|
Firstfruits

Pentecost

Trumpets
|
Atonement
|
Tabernacles

The Spiritual Significance of these Events

All of these physical pictures of covenant, relationship, law, and fellowship are natural shadows of what came to be spiritual realities fifty days after Christ's resurrection. First Christ ascended alone. But in just a few more days, He tells His disciples to expect the promised Spirit, the result of His finished work on the cross. After waiting and praying in the upper room for ten days (up until the celebration of the Jewish Feast of Pentecost), the Spirit of God was poured out upon all who believed. It is interesting how Luke begins the second chapter of Acts.

Acts 2:1 When the Day of Pentecost had fully come, they were all with one accord in one place.

But the literal translations of this verse are much clearer:

And in the fulfilling of the day of Pentecost (Greene's LitV)

And at the fulfillment of the day of Pentecost (Concordant Literal Translation)

And in the day of the Pentecost being fulfilled (Young's Literal Translation)

Two miraculous signs accompanied this event. There was a loud noise of a rushing wind—fulfilling the wind of

63

God's Spirit shown in Ezekiel's vision of dry bones. In Ezekiel's vision, the breath of God blew in and brought to life the "entire house of Israel."[43] The other manifestation was a small tongue of fire resting over the head of each believer. As the children of Israel camped in the wilderness, there was a pillar of fire over the tabernacle of God. At Pentecost, each of these believers had become the true tabernacle and eternal "dwelling place of God in the Spirit."[44]

The clear parallels between the old covenant shadows and the new covenant fulfillment are hard to miss. For instance, in fulfillment of the Exodus story, God has prepared us for this new covenant by causing us to participate in His three-day experience of death, burial, and resurrection. After their three days of purification, old covenant Israel had the blood of animal sacrifices physically sprinkled over those gathered at Sinai. In the new covenant, the blood of Christ works on behalf of all who believe.

Moses, Aaron, and the seventy elders went up the mountain to eat, drink, and see God. But now in Christ, all new covenant believers "eat His flesh and drink His blood,"[45] and by the revelation of the Spirit begin to see God face to face.[46] In the fulfillment of Pentecost, you could say that God descended upon the mountain in the form of His life-giving Spirit, or you could say that the new Israel was

---

[43] Ezekiel 37:11
[44] Ephesians 2:22
[45] John 6:53
[46] 2 Corinthians 3:18, 4:6

raised up and seated with Him on the mountain and in the cloud of His presence. Either way you describe it, the ones gathered in the upper room were suddenly given new life and invited up into Christ's relationship with His Father.

In the Exodus story, the covenant people were given the written law of God as the basis for their relationship. In Acts, these new covenant believers were given the "law of the Spirit of Life in Christ Jesus."[47] This new law is "written not with ink but by the Spirit of the living God, not on tablets of stone but on tablets of flesh, that is, of the heart."[48]

Formerly, the God of Israel was entirely un-approachable. There were boundaries established around His holy mountain as a clear sign that His presence was off-limits. But now, sin-laden Jews and Gentiles are baptized into the finished work of the cross, and the new, spiritual body of Christ is free to approach God without fear of condemnation. Now, from the Lord's point of view, flesh and sin have been put away, and there remains nothing left to judge. Hebrews 12 contrasts the approach to God in Exodus 24 with the fulfillment of these things *now* realized in Christ.

Heb 12:18 <u>*For you have not come to the mountain that may be touched*</u> *and that burned with fire, and to blackness and darkness and tempest, 19 and the sound of a trumpet and the voice of words, so that those who heard it begged*

---

[47] Romans 8:2

[48] 2 Corinthians 3:3

> *that the word should not be spoken to them anymore. 20 (For they could not endure what was commanded: "And if so much as a beast touches the mountain, it shall be stoned or shot with an arrow." 21 And so terrifying was the sight that Moses said, "I am exceedingly afraid and trembling.") 22 <u>But you have come to Mount Zion</u> and to the city of the living God, the heavenly Jerusalem, to an innumerable company of angels, 23 to the general assembly and church of the firstborn who are registered in heaven, to God the Judge of all, to the spirits of just men made perfect, 24 to Jesus the Mediator of the new covenant, and to the blood of sprinkling that speaks better things than that of Abel.*

You will notice that there is absolutely *nothing* mentioned in these verses that is said to be still in the future for the body of Christ. The inward realization of these realities is progressive as we permit the Spirit of Truth to "show us the things that have been freely given to us by God."[49] But the work is finished, and the free access is eternally secured. If you are a Christian, you *have come* to Mount Zion.

The Celebration of the Feast

While these events paint a vivid picture of Israel's entrance into covenant with God, the specific details of the

---

[49]   1 Corinthians 2:12

feast itself show us even more of God's perspective of the church's inclusion in Christ's finished work.

The most notable thing about the feast of Pentecost was the offering of the two loaves. Unlike any other grain offering offered to the Lord throughout the year, these were to be *leavened* loaves and *not* to be mixed with the customary oil and frankincense. It is a common, and I think accurate, interpretation to see these two loaves representing Jew and Gentile, equally weighed down with sin, lacking God's Spirit (without oil) and without any trace of the fragrance of Christ (frankincense).

> **Rom 3:9** *What then? Are we better than they? Not at all. For we have previously charged <u>both Jews and Greeks that they are all under sin</u>.*

Seeing God's work of salvation as the bringing together of two houses, or two groups, is a common theme throughout all of Scripture. When the one body of Israel divided into two groups, the northern ten tribes and the southern two tribes, God began to speak of His people as two entities that would one day be united again. Even after the Assyrians attacked, took captives, and assimilated the northern ten tribes into the surrounding gentile nations, God's prophets continued to speak of a great reconciliation between two houses. The prophets spoke as though God was counting the northern ten tribes together with all gentiles, and was promising a day when these peoples would be brought together with the Jews to make one new man under one Shepherd, one King, and in one Land.

These prophecies have led some Christians to expect a still future physical reunion and reconciliation between all twelve tribes. But the fulfillment of these prophecies is the incredible, eternal, and *spiritual* reality that Paul describes for us in Ephesians 2.

> **Eph 2:15** *Having abolished in His flesh the enmity, that is, the law of commandments contained in ordinances, <u>so as to create in Himself one new man from the two</u>, thus making peace, 16 and <u>that He might reconcile them both to God in one body through the cross</u>, thereby putting to death the enmity... <u>For through Him we both have access by one Spirit to the Father.</u>*

I believe these are the two leavened loaves represented in the Feast of Pentecost. In the ceremony, these two loaves were graciously joined to the perfect work of God in Christ. They are offered with seven perfect lambs, various burnt and peace offerings, and then waved before the Lord with two lambs. These loaves are *not* burned on the altar as a sweet smelling aroma unto God (like the usual daily grain offerings). God is not accepting these loaves in their current condition. Rather, they are given to the priest to eat. They are baptized into Christ, made partakers of His death, burial, and resurrection.

> **1 Cor 12:13** *For by one Spirit we were all baptized into one body—whether Jews or Greeks, whether*

slaves or free—and have all been made to drink into one Spirit.

Rom 6:3 *Or do you not know that as many of us as were baptized into Christ Jesus were baptized into His death?*

The Believer's Experience of Pentecost

As with the other feasts, Pentecost has a literal and historical event that corresponds to and manifests its fulfillment. Just as Passover, Unleavened Bread, and Firstfruits correspond to the literal death, burial, and resurrection of Christ, Pentecost was manifestly shown to be fulfilled when God poured out the long-awaited promise of His Spirit.

This being true, we must not miss the distinction between God's outward manifestation of Pentecost's fulfillment in Acts 2, and the individual believer's present experience of the *reality* of this fulfillment in the soul. As we have seen, every aspect of Pentecost that we have mentioned, both in the events that took place at Mount Sinai and the details of the feast itself, are realities of our relationship with God in Christ, and all of these must become present inward experiences as well.

We have already noted that the location and substance of all true fulfillment is Christ Himself. All prophecy is realized *in* Christ and *as* Christ, in one way or another. For this reason, the believer's experience of Pentecost fulfilled is not when they read and believe that Acts 2 took place, but rather when Christ in them makes all of these things living realities that faith knows and possesses.

It should be mentioned that although this feast deals with the inclusion of the church in the *already finished* work of God in Christ, this does not mean that believers get t o *skip* the experience of the first three feasts. In other words, just because the beginning of the church and its covenant with God is seen in feast number four, it does not follow that feast one, two, and three are only experienced by Christ. Quite the opposite is true. Just as soon as we are joined to Christ at Pentecost, His Passover becomes *our* death, His burial becomes *our* separation from the nature of sin, and His resurrection becomes *our* experience of being raised with Him to walk in newness of life. In both the shadow and the fulfillment, the church (Israel) is joined to Christ *after* He completes His work. However, in both shadow and fulfillment, Israel must learn to "keep the feasts" of Passover, Unleavened Bread, and Firstfruits, thus personally experiencing these realities.

Pentecost Brings an Understanding of the Body

Another way that the Lord causes us to experience the fulfillment of this feast is by revealing the reality of His church in us. This feast has much to show us about God's perspective of Christ's body.

We see, for instance, that sinful Jew and Gentile (the two loaves) are baptized into the same death and become one in the High Priest. As Paul describes in several of his letters, there are now no fleshly distinctions in Christ because there is no flesh in Christ. Jew, Gentile, male, female, slave, free—these are distinctions that have to do with physical bodies, places, and conditions, but have absolutely no relevance in the one new man that God has raised from the dead. The church is Christ, living in and glorifying Himself though the souls of those who have been born of His Spirit. In Him, all flesh has collided with the cross, fallen into the grave, and will never be seen again. The souls of every believer, however, are immediately made to drink of the same Spirit. Thus the body of Christ is not many human beings trying to please God in the flesh, but rather One resurrected Son living His life in many members (some still with earthly bodies and others without).

Furthermore, when we recognize that Pentecost is only feast number four and that there remain three more beyond it, we can understand that the salvation of the church is *not* God's ultimate purpose. On the contrary, the church was saved *for* a purpose. This is something that many in the church seem confused about. We often speak as though God's primary goal for humanity is that we *receive* the life that He offers. We talk about God's desire to get everybody saved. Please do not misunderstand me, the gift of life is an unspeakably great gift. But even in the natural realm we understand that receiving life does not define our purpose. We receive life *for* the purpose of growing up, maturing, reaching all of the potential that life has. This is true in the spiritual realm as well. The Lord certainly desires that all men be saved, but also that they come to the full knowledge of the truth.[50]   Receiving spiritual life is not our purpose. We are given life *for* a purpose, and that purpose has to do with bringing about a greater glory and harvest of God's true Seed.   This is precisely what we see described in the final three feasts.

Another extremely important thing that we can see through the biblical descriptions of this feast is the reality that the church has present (not merely future) access to the cloud of God's presence, the mountain of God's inheritance. We can *now*, in Christ, see the face of God and eat and drink with Him.   This is so important because in much of the Lord's body we speak as though these are future realties, ones that await the death of the body or the second coming.   The fact that natural eyes cannot see the Lord and physical hands do not touch Him, leads us to conclude that these pictures of union and communion await a greater day, a future consummation.   But nothing could be further from the truth. Physical eyes, bodies, and minds have *never* been the faculties that God designed for communion with Him. God is Spirit; therefore our experience of Him is present, spiritual, and takes place in the place or faculty that God has designed both to know Him and to be His dwelling place—the human soul.

---

[50]   1 Timothy 2:4

Chapter VI
The Feast of Trumpets

Key Scriptures: *Exod 19:13; Lev 23:23-25; Num 29:1-7; Neh 8:1-10; Isa 27:13;*

The Feast of Trumpets is the first of the fall feasts, and begins on the first day of the seventh month. The scriptures say very little about this feast. The most noteworthy feature is that this day is set apart as a day for the blowing of trumpets.

Lev 23:23 Then the LORD spoke to Moses, saying, 24 "Speak to the children of Israel, saying: 'In the seventh month, on the first day of the month, you shall have a sabbath-rest, a memorial of blowing of trumpets, a holy convocation. 25 You shall do no customary work on it; and you shall offer an offering made by fire to the LORD.' "

> **Num 29:1** *And in the seventh month, on the first day of the month, you shall have a holy convocation.* *You shall do no customary work.* <u>*For you it is a day of blowing the trumpets.*</u>

The blowing of trumpets is used throughout Scriptures to *call* God's people. Various types of trumpet blasts were used to get the attention of Israel: to gather or invite them together, to warn or announce something, or to call them to battle. The general idea is always related to Israel's call.

The blowing of trumpets during the Feast of Trumpets was understood in Jewish history as a call to turn, to repent, to prepare for the Day that was coming. (The Day of Atonement, which came ten days later, was usually referred to as simply "The Day.") Nothing more happened on this particular day. But the idea seems to be that one could not really expect to benefit from or experience the greatness of the coming Day if they did not first heed the call of the trumpet and humble their heart before the Lord.

The Spiritual Significance of Trumpets

Because I see the last three feasts collectively as a picture of God's objective or purpose for His people, it makes sense that the Feast of Trumpets represents God's call to the soul of the believer to "press on towards the goal of the high calling of God in Christ Jesus."[51] It is one thing to be joined to Christ at Pentecost. It is another thing to

---

[51]   Philippians 3:14

heed the call of God towards the end for which we were created. We see a clear picture of this in the Exodus from Egypt. Millions entered into the covenant with God at Mt. Sinai, but very few were willing to heed God's call to enter the Promised Land. Millions in Israel received the Lord as their God, having their own man-centered purposes for Him. But of that first generation, only Joshua and Caleb were willing to let God lead them into His eternal purpose for them.

As we will see, the Day of Atonement represents the access whereby we "draw near to God" (in spiritual comprehension or faith, *not* in physical proximity). Our experience of this day is one of both joy and judgment, glad union of the soul, and strict rejection of the flesh. But in order to move forward towards this day (a day that progressively dawns in our hearts), we need to humble our hearts and afflict our souls at the blast of God's trumpet. For us in the new covenant, this is an inward call, an invitation to the soul.

Trumpets in the Old Testament

Trumpets were used throughout Israel's history to gather the people of Israel together, to proclaim battle, and to announce certain sacrifices. Though not part of the actual feast day itself, there are several scriptures involving trumpets that I think can help us understand what this feast represents.

One such example takes place in Exodus 19 during the events surrounding the first Pentecost. We have already discussed how God descended upon the mountain and told Moses to set up boundary markers around the mountain. Israel did not have access to the cloud of God's presence. However, there is an interesting use of the trumpet involved in this story that helps us understand its spiritual significance.

> **Exod 19:12** *You shall set bounds for the people all around, saying, 'Take heed to yourselves that you do not go up to the mountain or touch its base. Whoever touches the mountain shall surely be put to death. 13 Not a hand shall touch him, but he shall surely be stoned or shot with an arrow; whether man or beast, he shall not live.' <u>When the trumpet sounds long, they shall come near the mountain.</u>*

The literal translation of verse 13 is even better. "At the sounding of the ram's horn, they shall *go up into the mountain*." Here we can see a direct correlation between the sounding of the trumpet and Israel's invitation to approach or ascend to God. The trumpet was the call, the sound of God's invitation to draw near.

Another example is found in Joel 2. In this chapter we again see the trumpet being used to call or invite God's people to "turn to Him with all their heart."[52] But there is another element involved here as well. In this chapter, the

---

[52] Joel 2:13

blowing of the trumpet is announcing two things or perhaps two sides of the same coin. The trumpet announces a "great *and* terrible day." It is both a day of drawing near to God and a day in which the enemies of God will be utterly destroyed. It is a day of rending garments and returning to the Lord your God, but it is also a day of darkness, gloom, and great judgment.

In the verse below, we see a trumpet call announcing the judgment of God's enemies.

> ***Joel 2:1*** *"Blow the trumpet in Zion, And sound an alarm in My holy mountain! Let all the inhabitants of the land tremble; For the day of the LORD is coming, For it is at hand: 2 A day of darkness and gloominess, A day of clouds and thick darkness..."*

However, in the verse below we see a trumpet call inviting Israel to humble their hearts and draw near to God

> ***Joel 2:15*** *Blow the trumpet in Zion, Consecrate a fast, Call a sacred assembly; 16 Gather the people, Sanctify the congregation, Assemble the elders, Gather the children and nursing babes.*

I find these two aspects of the trumpet call interesting because, in my experience, the Lord's call to go on with Him always involves these two realities. When I am heeding the call of God to grow up in Christ, there is always a tremendous cutting away in my heart of all that stands opposed to the Lord. Just like the types and shadows in the stories of King David, my soul is like a land that has received its true king; but in the land still dwells many uncircumcised enemies. So as I hear and humble my heart at the sound of God's trumpet, the result involves both the cutting down of uncircumcised flesh along with a greater awareness and experience of the King.

Another interesting Scripture that I believe can be tied to the Feast of Trumpets is found in Nehemiah 8. This chapter tells the story of Israel gathering together and hearing the words of God's law for the first time since returning from Babylonian captivity. Though there is no mention of trumpets in this chapter, this story takes place on the first day of the seventh month, the day of the Feast of Trumpets. On this day, Ezra the priest and scribe stands up before all the people to read and explain the law of God.

> **Neh 8:1** <u>Now all the people gathered together as one man</u> in the open square that was in front of the Water Gate; and they told Ezra the scribe to bring the Book of the Law of Moses, which the LORD had commanded Israel. 2 So Ezra the priest brought the Law before the assembly of men and women and all who could hear with understanding <u>on the first day of the seventh month</u>.

On this day, the reading of God's words was like a trumpet blast to souls of the men and women who gathered together. It touched them so deeply that they all began to weep and mourn—"For all the people wept, when they heard the words of the Law."[53] Eventually, Ezra encouraged them to stop their weeping and rejoice because of all that God had done for them.

I doubt it is coincidence that this deep call to the heart of Israel took place on the day of the Feast of Trumpets. Like the other Scriptures we have looked at, the focus here again seems to be that God is calling to hearts. He is getting the attention of those in Israel who gathered before Him as one man.

---

[53]   Nehemiah 8:9

Chapter VII
The Day of Atonement

Key Scriptures: *Lev 16:1-34, 23:26-32; Num 29:7; Zech 3:1-10; Heb 4:16, 7:19, 7:25, 10:1-2, 10:22*

The Day of Atonement was the sixth yearly feast in Israel. It took place on the tenth day of the seventh month. The ceremony involved in the Day of Atonement is perhaps more involved than all of the other feasts. The entire chapter of Leviticus 16 describes the details of this day.

In summary, this is the day where the priest made *atonement* for the tabernacle of God using the blood of a bull and of a goat. The ceremony went as follows. First, the High Priest washed his entire body in pure water and put on the pure linen garments which were specifically said to prevent flesh from being seen.

Exod 28:42 *And you shall make for them linen trousers <u>to cover their nakedness</u>; they shall reach from the waist to the thighs. 43 They shall be on Aaron and on his sons when they come into the* *tabernacle of meeting, or when they come near the altar to minister in the holy place, that they do not incur iniquity and die. It shall be a statute forever to him and his descendants after him.*

A bull was brought before the Lord and the High Priest confessed his personal sin and the sins of his house (the Levites) over this animal. The animal was then killed, and its blood was put into a basin. Two goats were then brought before the Lord from the congregation. Lots were then cast for the goats, and one is chosen to be offered to the Lord; the other is chosen as *azazel*—a Hebrew word that means either Satan or complete removal (there is some debate about this). After this selection, the High priest takes hot coals from the brazen altar, puts them into a censer, then takes a handful of holy incense and goes into the tabernacle beyond both veils. He sets the burning censer before the ark, throws the incense onto the burning coals, and lets the smoke fill up the Holy of Holies.

The high priest then goes out of the tabernacle, retrieves the basin with the bull's blood, and enters back into the tabernacle beyond the veil. He sprinkles the blood both on, and in front of, the Ark of the Covenant, and then exits. He then kills the goat that was chosen for the Lord, takes its blood back into the tabernacle, and does the same with its blood as he did with the blood of the bull. The High Priest then mixes the blood of the bull with the blood of the goat and sprinkles them both on and around the incense altar that is before the veil.

Finally, the priest exits the tabernacle and goes over to the living goat dedicated to *azazel*. He lays his hands on the head of this goat, confesses over it all of the iniquities and transgressions of Israel, and sends the goat away to an uninhabited land never to be seen again. The bodies of the bull and the goat are then dragged outside of the camp and burned.

Common Interpretations of The Day of Atonement

Nearly every book, commentary, and article I have read concerning the Day of Atonement links this feast with one of two things: 1) most commonly, a still future day of the Lord, a day of judgment coming to the earth or, 2) the sacrifice of Christ on the cross, the forgiveness of sins, and the fact that Christ brings us to His Father behind the veil.

The great majority of contemporary books, articles, and websites connect the last three feasts to end-times events. It is thought by many that Trumpets corresponds to the rapture, the Day of Atonement speaks of the great judgment day to come, and Tabernacles is a picture of the Millennium, or a coming new heaven and earth.

From what I have already said, it is obviously my belief that any future interpretation of the feasts of Israel is nonsensical for a variety of reasons. First, because "the eternal purpose of God has been accomplished in Christ Jesus."[54] Second, because although the fulfillment of types and shadows often has a natural manifestation, the

---

[54] Ephesians 3:11

fulfillment itself is always spiritual, eternal, and in Christ. It bears repeating that Christ Himself, and our eternal spiritual union with Him, is the fulfillment, realization, and reality of all that God has ever spoken, promised, or prefigured. Third, because the authors of the New Testament speak of these feasts as present spiritual realities in Christ.

The other interpretation (namely that the Day of Atonement represents Christ's death on the cross, the forgiveness of sin, and Christ bringing us to His Father behind the veil) is not altogether wrong, but I believe it is unsatisfactory for several reasons. For instance, if the Day of Atonement simply represents the death of Christ on the cross and our forgiveness of sins, then why is it the *sixth* feast? Why was it not the *first*? Do we not already have an incredible picture of the death, burial, and resurrection of Christ, and the covenant based on this finished work, given to us in the first feasts?

Furthermore, if the High Priest represents Christ bringing us once for all behind the veil to His Father, then why did he wear only the white linens on this day? On the Day of Atonement, the High Priest took off his customary garments that represented the entire house of Israel, with the twelve stones and the twelve names of the tribes. And if going into the Holy of Holies represents Christ's return to the Father, why did the priest go in and out several times? And why was the scapegoat sent away only after he exited the tabernacle for the final time? Or, if going into the Holy of Holies represented Christ's three-day journey into death and judgment, followed by His return in resurrection, why then do we see the Ark and the cloud of glory in the place that supposedly represents death and separation from God? These questions left me puzzled and led me to search for a fuller understanding of what God is showing us in this feast.

My View of the Day of Atonement

It makes more sense to me that the Day of Atonement speaks primarily of *the access or approach* that God made available to His people through Christ. It is a day in which God's house is made fully and freely accessible by way of atonement. A way is provided by which we can approach God, and this approach implies a great division. Even as the blood of one goat is brought behind the veil and the other goat is completely removed (Heb. *azazel*), so too in the experience of each believer, keeping this feast involves both an incredible invitation to draw near and an unyielding rejection of all that is not Christ.

There are several reasons why I believe this. The first is because this is the *sixth* feast, not the first. Christ has already returned to God in Firstfruits, and brought us to God in Pentecost. Now, in the seventh month, those who have been joined to God by covenant are invited to draw near to Him. Much more will be said about this below.

The second reason is the fact that the overarching theme of Leviticus 16 is the wrong versus the right approach to God. All of Leviticus 16 deals with the Day of Atonement, but notice how the chapter begins.

Lev 16:1 *Now the LORD spoke to Moses after the death of the two sons of Aaron, when they offered profane fire before the LORD, and died; 2 and the LORD said to Moses: "<u>Tell Aaron your brother not to come at just any time into the Holy Place inside the veil, before the mercy seat which is on the ark, lest he die</u>; for I will appear in the cloud above the mercy seat. 3 "Thus (in this way!) Aaron shall come into the Holy Place."*

The chapter begins with God explaining that the two sons of Aaron (who were consumed with fire) approached God in the *wrong* way. They cannot draw near to Him at just any time or in just any way. In new covenant language, this is like pointing out that Adam, the wrong man, cannot draw near to God. There is a very specific way, time, and place to approach God, and Christ is all three. Christ is the way that God has provided by which we can experience life behind the veil. The remainder of Leviticus 16 describes this way.

The third reason has to do with the definition of the word atonement. This is the Hebrew word which means *cover*. So judging simply by the meaning of the word, the Day of Atonement does not seem to point to the initial day of our baptism into Christ's death, the forgiveness for sins, or a day of judgment still to come. The Day of Atonement was a yearly *covering* that allowed a daily approach. Below we will look at these reasons in more detail.

Atonement — A Covering

Part of our interpretation of this day hinges on our understanding of this word atonement. Many authors treat this word as though it simply means forgiveness, others as though it refers to a satisfaction or an amends made for a wrong. While there may be some truth in these definitions, these are in fact acquired and interpretive definitions that really do not do justice to the Hebrew word.

The Hebrew word translated atonement is *kaphar* and it quite simply means to cover over. In the Old Testament, this same word is often translated "lid" with reference to the Ark of the Covenant (though many translations translate this word as "mercy seat" for no etymological reason).

> *Exod 25:17 You shall make a <u>mercy seat [Heb. kaphar—covering]</u> of pure gold; two and a half cubits shall be its length and a cubit and a half its width.*

This same word is used as a verb in the following verse from Genesis.

> *Gen 6:14 Make yourself an ark of gopherwood; make rooms in the ark, and cover it [Heb. kaphar] inside and outside with pitch.*

The idea of a covering is one that appears over and over again in the types and shadows of the Old Testament. The concept of covering is much more than merely the idea that

God covers up our sins, buries them, and keeps them out of sight. Again, there are shreds of truth in this idea, but I believe a much better definition of God's covering can be derived from many types and shadows in the Old Testament. It seems to me that the concept of covering consistently represents how the believer is covered with Christ in such a way that for God to relate to what is covered with Christ is to relate to Christ Himself.

Consider the following Old Testament illustrations. After believing the lie and eating the forbidden fruit, Adam and Eve try to cover their nakedness with fig leaves. In one of the first pictures of the work of the cross in the Bible, God covers them in animal skins, not only removing the problem of nakedness, but relating with them based upon the life of another.

Noah's ark is covered (*kaphar*) in pitch, and becomes the vessel in which all of Noah's family experiences God's judgment with him. Everything that joins Noah in the ark is collectively seen and recognized as belonging to Christ Himself in His death, burial, and resurrection. Water could not penetrate this covering to destroy it. And on the other side of God's great judgment, all that had entered into the ark with Noah came out with him as a new creation in covenant with God.

> **Gen 7:23** *So He destroyed all living things which were on the face of the ground: both man and cattle, creeping thing and bird of the air. They were destroyed from the earth. Only Noah and those who were with him in the ark remained alive.*

After the flood, God offers this new creation the covering of a rainbow. With this covering He gives the promise that His wrath is spent, judgment is over, and He will never more destroy what He has already judged. God recognizes Noah and his family according to His finished work. So when Noah foolishly gets drunk and uncovers himself, his two wiser sons walk backwards and cover their father with a blanket, refusing to look upon a nakedness that God no longer recognizes.

When Isaac desires to bless his son, Rebecca covers Jacob in the clothes, skin, and the smell of the firstborn. When Jacob appears to his father, he is recognized, kissed, and blessed as the true heir.

There are many other examples: Rachel's idols are covered with blood and not found by either Laban or Jacob; the High Priest was covered in pure linen from head to toe, even putting on "linen underpants" so that "no flesh was seen when he ascended the altar;"[55] Moses was hidden in the cleft of the rock and covered with God's hand when he drew near to experience God's glory, etc.

The point in all of these pictures of the covering seems to be that, in one way or another, God applies His perspective of Christ to the person or thing being covered, thereby 1) purifying it from all that is not Christ, 2) giving to it that which belongs to Christ, and 3) relating to it as Christ Himself. Of course this has the effect of removing sin from the picture and reconciling the person with God, but the

---

[55] Exodus 20:26

greater reality is that God is now relating to whatever He has covered with Christ as Christ Himself.[56]

In the case of the Day of Atonement, God fully covered His house so that He was entirely accessible (in an old covenant, type and shadow way) to those who wanted to draw near. As always, this atonement was accomplished by Christ in the one-time, finished work of the cross. But as with all of the feasts, this day becomes the subjective experience of each believer as we draw near to God. The Day of Atonement made perfect access, removed the barriers, opened the way, and purified the place where we live together with the Lord. But now *this* reality of the cross must become our present experience and our perpetual desire.

Drawing Near to God

As mentioned previously, this *approach to God* seems to be the real focus of this day. The two sons of Aaron drew near to God in the wrong way, but God provided a way for Israel to draw near to Him.

The concept of drawing near or approaching God appears several times in the New Testament, mostly in the book of Hebrews because this book explains the fulfillment of the Old Covenant priesthood. Like any other spiritual

---

[56] Of course this doesn't mean that we become Christ, or possess divinity in ourselves. But as those who are baptized into Christ's death, and come to live in and by Christ's resurrection, we are the body of Christ, the ones "accepted in the Beloved," and we come to share His relationship with His Father.

reality, this concept is easily misunderstood and misapplied by the natural mind. It has absolutely nothing to do with physical proximity or with relational closeness or distance. God is eternally present, perfectly accessible, and joined by Christ to the soul of every true believer. In terms of proximity or union, it is impossible for a Christian to get closer to God. Whether we are in the body or out of the body, "those who have been joined to the Lord have become one spirit with Him." [57]

Drawing near to God therefore refers to the inward process whereby the soul of the believer comes to a true and living consciousness of God, a real knowing of Him, and a corresponding "cleansing of our consciences"[58] with regard to all that is contrary to Him. It is a drawing near in spiritual knowledge, familiarity, and acknowledgment that always includes the leaving behind of our "consciousness of sins."[59]

The Approach Described in Scripture

Like all types and shadows in the Old Testament, the access to God secured on the Day of Atonement and the approach into the Holy of Holies, has a spiritual fulfillment in the new covenant. The believer, now clothed in Christ, has free access to experience the fullness of God's gift of life. This is the greatness of our calling, the invitation to know

---

[57] 1 Corinthians 6:17
[58] Hebrews 9:14, 10:22
[59] Hebrews 10:2

and experience the "deep things of God."[60] Drawing near to God is therefore connected in Scripture to our *expectation*. The possibility of a conscious knowing of God, a true experience of union, and a deep familiarity with Christ as our very life should be the motivating expectation of every Christian's heart. Notice how this expectation is described in the verses below.

> **Heb 7:19** *For the law made nothing perfect; on the other hand, there is the bringing in of a better hope, [Lit. expectation[61]] through which we draw near to God.*

> **Phil 3:8** *Yet indeed I also count all things loss for the excellence of the knowledge of Christ Jesus my Lord, for whom I have suffered the loss of all things, and count them as rubbish, that I may gain Christ.*

In other verses, drawing near to God is connected to our taking possession of what God has already given us, or laying hold of the salvation that we already have. This is an accurate way to describe how we grow up in Christ. Spiritual growth is never the progressive acquisition of something that we do not have. Rather, it is the progressive

---

[60] 1 Corinthians 2:10

[61] The Greek word *elpis* is unfortunately usually translated hope in the New Testament. Nevertheless, the meaning of this Greek word has to do with the expectation of something certain, and not the wishful-thinking implied by the word hope. Any Greek lexicon will confirm this.

discovery and experience of all that God *has* given to us in Christ.[62] The land of Israel, for example, was given to Israel before they even crossed the Jordan River. But all that God had already given to Israel had to be possessed by faith. The verses below describe this reality in the language of drawing near to God.

> **Heb 7:25** *And from this He is able to <u>save to the uttermost the ones drawing near to God through Him</u>, forever living to intercede on their behalf.*

> **Heb 4:16** *Therefore, let us draw near with confidence to the throne of grace, that we may receive [or take] mercy, and we may find grace for timely help.*

This last verse is easily misunderstood. The point of Hebrews 4:16 is not that we approach God once in a while and ask for a little help. The idea here is that this same approach is how we possess (take, discover, perceive) what is now available at the true mercy seat of God.

In still other verses, drawing near to God is connected with the purification of the believer, elsewhere called the cleansing of the conscience. Notice the implications of the verses below.

> **Heb 10:1** *For the law, having a shadow of the good things to come, and not the very image of the things, can never with these same sacrifices, which*

---

[62] 1 Corinthians 2:12

> *they offer continually year by year, <u>make those</u>*
> *<u>who approach perfect</u>. 2 For then would they not*
> *have ceased to be offered? For the worshipers, once*
> *purified, <u>would have had no more consciousness of</u>*
> *<u>sins</u>.*

The comparison presented in Hebrews 10:1-2 is between the shadow and the substance. The point is that the substance (unlike the shadow) is an approach to God that has the potential to "make perfect" and to remove the believer's "consciousness of sins." This is clearly the implication of the following verses as well.

> **Heb 10:19** *Therefore, brethren, having boldness*
> *to enter the Holiest by the blood of Jesus, 20 <u>by a</u>*
> *<u>new and living way which He consecrated for us,</u>*
> *<u>through the veil, that is, His flesh</u>, 21 and having a*
> *High Priest over the house of God, 22 <u>let us draw</u>*
> *<u>near with a true heart in full assurance of faith,</u>*
> *<u>having our hearts sprinkled from an evil con-</u>*
> *<u>science and our bodies washed with pure water</u>.*

> **James 4:8** *Draw near to God and He will draw*
> *near to you. Cleanse your hands, you sinners; and*
> *purify your hearts, you double-minded.*

In each of these verses that connect drawing near to God with purification, I think we see the fulfillment of the two goats from the Day of Atonement. On the same day, in the same ceremony, one goat is brought near into the Holy of Holies, and the *result* is the absolute removal of the other goat. Lots were drawn and one goat was chosen to be "for the Lord." The other goat was chosen to be *azazel*— meaning either complete removal, or representing the Hebrew name of Satan.[63] Both of these realities take place in the heart of the believer who is drawing near to God. The measure of Christ working in the soul is always recognized, accepted, and enlarged. The measure of sin that still works through the unrenewed mind is, as a result, removed from the camp.

The order of how the priest dealt with the two goats is significant. The entering in with the blood of the one is *followed by* the removal of the other. In other words, our drawing near to God is the cause; the cleansing of the conscience is the effect. The decrease of the wrong man is *always* the byproduct of Christ's increase in the soul. It is never the other way around. Sadly, many Christians try to fight against and free themselves from the flesh, hoping for Christ's increase as a result. This will never happen. John the Baptist gave us the correct order when he said, "He must increase; I must decrease."[64]

Still another important aspect of this approach mentioned in Scriptures is the fact that drawing near to God is done *by faith* and not by any religious action or work. We must understand that faith is not beliefs that reside in our mind.[65] It is not our ideas or convictions about

---

[63] For me the debate between the meaning of this Hebrew word is a dead issue because, with both definitions, the implication is a total contrariness to and separation from God.

[64] John 3:30

[65] There are many other MSF publications and teachings that deal

spiritual things.   Faith is something purely spiritual, something that comes from God that causes us to know God.   Christ is said to be the "Author and Finisher of our faith."[66]   Faith is not man's understanding of spiritual things but rather the Spirit's understanding of all things working in the soul of man.   So when the mind, light, perspective (faith!) of the Son of God is operating in the human soul, what is real to the Head progressively becomes real to the members of the body as well.   It is in this way that we walk by faith and not by sight.   And it is in this way that we draw near to God by faith.

> **Heb 10:22** *Let us draw near with a true heart in full assurance of faith.*

> **Heb 11:6** *But without faith it is impossible to please God. For it is right that the one drawing near to God should believe[67]* [verb form of the Greek word faith] *that He is, and that He becomes a rewarder to the ones seeking Him out.*

Under the old covenant, drawing near to God was possible only in a natural, type-and-shadow, kind of way. While the first tabernacle or temple was still standing (that is, while the first covenant was still the way God was

---

with the reality of faith in detail.

[66]   Hebrews 12:2

[67]   When you see the word "believe" in the New Testament, it is the same Greek word for faith (*pistis*) in the form of a verb. Because English does not have a verb form for the word faith, we use the word believe instead.

relating to man) God had not yet opened up the true approach by which we actually approach Him and live with Him behind the veil. This is precisely what the author of Hebrews tells us.

> **Heb 9:6** *Now when these things had been thus prepared, the priests always went into the first part of the tabernacle, performing the services. 7 But into the second part the high priest went alone once a year, not without blood, which he offered for himself and for the people's sins committed in ignorance; 8 <u>the Holy Spirit indicating this, that the way into the Holiest of All was not yet made manifest while the first tabernacle was still standing.</u> 9 It was symbolic for the present time in which both gifts and sacrifices are offered which <u>cannot make him who performed the service perfect in regard to the conscience</u>— 10 concerned only with foods and drinks, various washings, and fleshly ordinances imposed until the time of reformation. 11 But Christ came as High Priest of the good things to come, with the greater and more perfect tabernacle not made with hands, that is, not of this creation.*

The White Garments of the Priest

Generally it is assumed that the white garments of the High Priest on the Day of Atonement represent Christ in

His purity or holiness approaching God behind the veil on our behalf. I have already mentioned some problems with that interpretation. For the reasons we have mentioned, it seems more fitting to see the priest in His white linen garments *not* as a picture of Christ entering God's presence on our behalf but rather the church or the believer approaching God clothed in Christ.

In both cases Christ is the focus. He, not us, is the means of approach, the One securing the relationship. It is only by His merit, His work, His righteousness that we have access to God. However, the specific focus of this feast seems to me to be that of the church's approach to God in Christ and not Christ's approach to God on behalf of the church.

Every day of the year the high priest wore the normal priestly garments with the breastplate, the stones, the gold, etc.—all representing the twelve tribes of Israel gathered up into one Man, finding access to God in Him. Very regularly, the High Priest would enter into these holy places with all of Israel hidden in Him "now to appear in the presence of God on behalf of us."[68] But this garment was *removed* during the Day of Atonement in order to paint for us another picture of the priestly work of Christ, the other side of the same coin. Again, there are no contradictions between these two views of Christ's work. Rather, they are two perspectives of the same reality. Throughout the year, with the twelve tribes bound to his breastplate, the High Priest brought the church into the presence of God. But in this particular feast, I believe we see a picture of the

---

[68] Hebrews 9:24

church's approach to God having been clothed in Christ's resurrected life.

There are several things that seem to support the idea that the priest in his white linen represents the church's approach in Christ. First of all, there are other verses in the Bible that associate the cleansing or changing of clothing with "putting on Christ," and subsequently approaching the Lord. We saw this in our discussion of Pentecost. When Israel was preparing to approach the Lord on Mt. Sinai, they were told to prepare themselves for three days, purify themselves, and *wash their clothing*. The purifying of their clothing represented a new covering in which they were then able to approach the mountain.

Furthermore, before Aaron went into the Tabernacle on the Day of Atonement, he had to wash his body in pure water. According to Jewish tradition, he was also sprinkled with the ashes of the red heifer mixed with water on the third and seventh day before the feast, just in case he had unknowingly become unclean. With this in mind, look again at Hebrews 10:22. This verse seems to clearly connect the approach of Aaron with the experience of the *believer*.

> **Heb 10:22** <u>Let us</u> draw near with a true heart in full assurance of faith, <u>having our hearts sprinkled</u> from an evil conscience and <u>our bodies washed with pure water</u>.

Clearly Aaron's preparation for drawing near to God is *not* being compared with Christ's return to the Father but rather with *our* approach (let us draw near) to God in Christ. We are the ones said to be experiencing this washing, sprinkling, and the drawing near to God through Christ.

The New Testament frequently encourages us to put on Christ, or to clothe ourselves in Christ, as a way of describing our ever-increasing experience of His Life. By putting on Christ we are coming to see and know Him as our life, our covering, our righteousness, our light, as well as our relationship in the Spirit to other members of His body.

> **Rom 13:14** *But put on the Lord Jesus Christ, and make no provision for the flesh, to fulfill its lusts.*

> **Col 3:10** *And having put on the new man who is renewed in knowledge according to the image of Him who created him...*

Tying this in with the Feast of Atonement, it would make more sense that *we* are the ones in need of these pure linen garments. We need to be clothed in Christ, to know Him as our purity and righteousness, and as our relationship with God where none of our flesh or nakedness is seen.

Finally, there are several places in Scripture where the bride of Christ or the individual believer is spoken of as having been given new, clean garments as the requirement for approaching the Lord. We have referenced Exodus 28, where the use of linen garments is clearly connected with *our* flesh being covered with Christ.

> **Exod 28:42** *And you shall make for them linen trousers <u>to cover their nakedness</u>; they shall reach from the waist to the thighs. 43 They shall be on Aaron and on his sons when they come into the tabernacle of meeting, or <u>when they come near</u> the altar to minister in the holy place, that they do not incur iniquity and die.*

In a multitude of verses in Leviticus, cleaning the body and the clothes was how individual Israelites who had become unclean were restored to fellowship with the Tabernacle and with the camp. In Ezekiel 44, white linen garments are again given to us as a picture of being clothed in Christ in such a way that removes flesh from the relationship, and allows us to draw near to God.

> **Ezek 44:16** *"They shall enter My sanctuary, and they shall come near My table to minister to Me, and they shall keep My charge. 17 And it shall be, whenever they enter the gates of the inner court, that <u>they shall put on linen garments</u>; no wool shall come upon them while they minister within the gates of the inner court or within the house. 18 <u>They shall have linen turbans on their heads and linen trousers on their bodies</u>; they shall not clothe themselves with anything that causes sweat.*

In Zechariah 3, Zechariah has a vision of Joshua the high priest brought before the Lord in filthy garments. Satan accuses him, but the Lord removes his filthy garments and clothes him in clean clothes from head to toe. Now covered in clean clothes, Joshua is promised *access* into the heavenly court. Afterward, the Lord explains that His Servant the Branch (the Messiah) is coming and will make all of this possible by removing the iniquity of the land in one day.

All of these verses seem to me to support the idea that the High Priest's approach to God on the Day of Atonement speaks of the believer's access to the Lord. Christ's body, (the church) fully clothed in Christ, has been washed and sprinkled, and now the invitation of the Spirit of God is "Let us draw near with a true heart in full assurance of faith."

The Day

To the ancient Jews the Day of Atonement was called "The Great Day" or often simply just "The Day." In the Talmud (the ancient book of commentaries, interpretations, and traditions of the Jewish sages) this feast is also simply referred to as "The Day."

There seems to be an undeniable connection between the usage of the word "day" in Scripture and the events associated with the Day of Atonement. The biblical descriptions (especially in the Prophets) of "the Lord's day" or the "day of the Lord" seem almost always to involve both a drawing near to God and a terrible judgment of what the

Lord rejects. Joel says, "For the day of the Lord is great and very terrible; Who can endure it?"[69]

Throughout the prophets, there is perhaps no other theme as predominant as the coming day of the Lord. Christians are usually quick to assume this day to be a natural period of time, but the enormous quantity of scriptures describing the reality of the Lord's Day simply cannot be reconciled with a natural, temporal inter-pretation. From the Lord's perspective (given to us in Genesis 1:5), the word "day" has to do with the presence of light and the subsequent effects of that light on God's creation. "God called the light day,"[70] But He did not call the first twenty-four hours day.

Even a quick read-through of the prophetic books will reveal that the Lord's promised day always has two very distinguishable aspects. It is a day of judgment, wrath, and destruction; it is also a day of salvation, blessing, and reward.

I do not doubt that the spiritual reality of this day has physical, natural manifestations associated with it. For example, in the events surrounding the desolation of Israel and the destruction of Jerusalem in 70 AD, natural Israel (Israel in the flesh, the physical seed that had rejected their Messiah) was literally and physically destroyed by the Roman Empire. The other Israel (spiritual Israel, sons of Abraham by faith) was protected and gathered up by the Lord "into His barn."[71] Many Christians expect similar

---

[69] Joel 2:11
[70] Genesis 1:5
[71] Matthew 13:30

external manifestations in the future. As far as I am concerned, as long as we are talking about *manifestation* and not *fulfillment,* there is no need to argue about these things.

However, the spiritual *fulfillment* of this day cannot be bound to time or events. The true Day of the Lord could never be contained by the natural realm. This is a spiritual day that involves the dawning of spiritual light, made available through the resurrection of Jesus Christ. It is therefore a day that "dawns in the heart."[72] We become "sons of the day,"[73] learn to "walk in the day."[74] We are judged "not by a human day" (1 Cor 4:3 literal translation), but rather the Day of the Lord "declares each man's work."[75] In the light of this Day, we experience in ourselves both the drawing near to God, and the great rejection of the adamic man.

The Fulfillment of This Feast

In summary, the fulfillment of the Day of Atonement is the inward, spiritual approach unto God whereby we come into His presence and leave all but Christ behind. Atonement was perfected in the finished work of Christ on the cross, but our approach is an ongoing, progressive drawing near to God in the soul by faith. This drawing near

---

[72] 2 Peter 1:19
[73] 1 Thessalonians 5:5
[74] Romans 13:13
[75] 1 Corinthians 3:13

is the process whereby the soul learns to live behind the veil and experience the absolute removal of all that God has rejected.

Chapter VIII
The Feast of Tabernacles (Booths, Ingathering)

Key Scriptures: *Exod 23:16, 34:22-23; Lev 23:33-43; Num 29:12-34; Deut 16:13-15; 1 Kgs 8:1-4; Zech 14:16-19; John 7:2-10, 37-39*

The Feast of Tabernacles (also called the Feast of Booths, or the Feast of The Ingathering) is the seventh and last feast in Israel's yearly calendar. The feast begins on the fifteenth day of the seventh month, five days after the Day of Atonement, and it lasts for one week. The first day of the feast was a holy convocation, and no customary work was permitted.   During the entire week there was a large number of burnt, sin, grain, and drink offerings offered up to the Lord each day. But the two most notable aspects of this final feast were 1) the gathering together of the harvest of the land along with various live branches and 2) the command that all of Israel had to construct small booths (Heb. *sukkot*) and live in them for the week.

There was a difference in interpretation between the Pharisees and the Sadducees with regard to some of the details of this feast. The Sadducees believed that the booths were to be constructed out of the fruit and live branches that were gathered together for the feast. The Pharisees believed that the fruits of the land and the live branches were simply meant to be carried around, waved, and displayed before the Lord and that the booths were to be constructed of other types of branches. This was by far the predominant view during the time of Christ. Interestingly, because of the prophet Zechariah's connection between the coming Messianic salvation and the Feast of Tabernacles,[76] the Jews of Christ's day associated the waving of palm and other branches with the arrival of the Messiah. This is why many waved palm branches before Jesus as He rode into Jerusalem the week before He was crucified.

Common Interpretations of Tabernacles

As with the other two fall feasts, the great majority of writers associate this last feast with a still future event. Because of the emphasis on the gathering of the harvest, many see Tabernacles as a picture of a coming great end-times revival.   Others see it pointing to the gathering together of all Christians as the "harvest of souls" that God has always desired.

---

[76]   Zechariah 14

The aspect of dwelling in booths has been interpreted in a variety of different ways. Sadly, most see it as a still-future relationship of union with God that we are awaiting. Some believe this relationship begins during the so-called millennial reign of Christ, others that it awaits a future new heaven and earth.

My Interpretation of the Feast of Tabernacles

As I have already argued, I believe the last three feasts speak of the goal, objective, or purpose of God that He works out in His body, the church. Once again, although these realities may have various outward manifestations or expressions, I believe the true *fulfillment* of God's purpose is spiritual, eternal, and therefore invisible to the natural eye. As we have said several times, fulfillment is always some reality or aspect of Christ Himself. Therefore, fulfillment works in us to the measure that Christ is known by us and formed in us.

Because Tabernacles is the final feast and the seventh feast (a number that represents completion or totality), this feast paints a picture for us of the ultimate intention of God. We see in Tabernacles a view of Christ and His work that is both the realization of man's purpose and the perfect completion of God's eternal purpose.

From God's perspective, the body of Christ becomes the eternal increase and glory of the one Seed that died alone. At this feast "no man shall appear before the Lord empty-handed."[77]   Every Israelite bears some measure of Christ's increase and lives together with God as one.   We will say more about this shortly.   From man's perspective, Christ becomes our eternal dwelling place, our joy, our glory, and our great feast.

The Ingathering

All throughout the Old and New Testaments the Lord speaks of His eternal purpose in the language of a harvest. It is important to realize, from God's perspective, this harvest has *always* been the increase of His unique Seed. Just as Eve came out from Adam and was given back to him as his own increase, so too Israel/the church must come out *from* Christ (born of His life, filled with His life) and be given back to Him as His own increase.   Though the Lord certainly "desires all men to be saved and come to the full knowledge of the truth,"[78] He is never confused (like we are) about real versus plastic fruit.   The ingathering of God's harvest is the measure of His Seed formed in the soil of our hearts.

This ingathering is pictured in various ways throughout Scripture, and it is frequently shown to be the *result* of the Day of the Lord.   Again, the trumpets invite the soul to the great Day; the Day draws us behind the veil and separates us from all that is not Christ; then the ingathering shows us how God takes unto Himself the harvest of His Son in Israel. None of these things happen according to calendar dates or natural events. Natural time was only relevant in the old covenant. In the new covenant, all that God offers the soul of man is *now in Christ.* "Jesus Christ is the same yesterday, today, and forever."[79] Therefore, this ingathering is a perpetual harvest of Christ on God's eternal seventh day.

Jesus and the apostles referred to their generation as the firstfruits, or at times as the wheat harvest.[80] Wheat was the first of the summer crops to be harvested (followed by grapes, figs, pomegranates, olives, etc). The harvest continues forever because "of the increase of His government and peace there will be no end."[81] But the first generation of Christians was the first true increase of Christ in His body or kingdom.

> **Jas 1:18** *Of His own will He brought us forth by the word of truth, that we might be a kind of firstfruits of His creatures.*

> **John 4:35** *Behold, I say to you, lift up your eyes and look at the fields, for they are already white[82] for harvest!*

---

[79] Hebrews 13:8

[80] Matthew 3:12, 13:24-30; Luke 3:17

[81] Isaiah 9:7

[82] This was a direct reference to the wheat harvest, the firstfruits of the gospel's increase. When wheat was ready to harvest it turned from green to yellow or white.

The Ingathering Throughout Scripture

God's desire to gather together His people unto Himself appears all throughout Scripture and points to the same objective that we see pictured in the Feast of Tabernacles.

> ***Psa 50:5*** *Gather My saints together to Me, Those who have made a covenant with Me by sacrifice.*

Speaking to Zion, the Lord says,

> ***Isa 49:18*** *"Lift up your eyes, look around and see; All these gather together and come to you. As I live," says the LORD, "You shall surely clothe yourselves with them all as an ornament, And bind them on you as a bride does."*

> ***Isa 60:4*** *Lift up your eyes all around, and see: They all gather together, they come to you; Your sons shall come from afar, and your daughters shall be nursed at your side.*

> ***Eze 39:17*** *Assemble yourselves and come; Gather together from all sides to My sacrificial meal which I am sacrificing for you, a great sacrificial meal on the mountains of Israel, that you may eat flesh and drink blood.*

Other verses tie the ingathering of the Lord's harvest more directly to the Feast of Tabernacles. For instance, the dedication of Solomon's temple took place during the Feast of Tabernacles and paints a picture of all of Israel gathering unto their king. On that day, King Solomon first gathered together the ark and the other furniture from the tabernacle and set them in God's Temple.   Then, all of the men of Israel gathered to King Solomon.

> **1Kgs 8:1** <u>Then Solomon gathered</u> the elders of Israel, and all the heads of the tribes, the chief of the fathers of the sons of Israel, to King Solomon in Jerusalem, that they might bring up the ark of the covenant of Jehovah out of the city of David, which is Zion. 2 <u>And all the men of Israel were gathered to King Solomon</u>, in the month of Ethanim, <u>at the feast, which is the seventh month</u>. 3 And all the elders of Israel came in, and the priests lifted up the ark, 4 and brought up the ark of Jehovah, and the tabernacle of the congregation, and all the holy vessels that were in the tabernacle, even those the priests and the Levites brought.

Centuries later, Zechariah spoke of a day when the remnant from every nation that remained after God's judgment, would gather together before the Lord and keep the Feast of Tabernacles.

> **Zech 14:16** And it shall be, <u>everyone who is left from all the nations which came up against Jerusalem shall go up from year to year to worship the King, Jehovah of Hosts, and to keep the Feast of</u>

Tabernacles. *17 And it shall be, whoever will not go up from the families of the earth to Jerusalem to worship the King, Jehovah of Hosts, there shall even be no rain on them. 18 And if the family of Egypt does not go up, nor come in, then the rain shall not be on them, but the plague with which Jehovah shall strike the nations who do not come up to keep the Feast of Tabernacles. 19 This shall be Egypt's offense, and the offense of all nations who do not come up to keep the Feast of Tabernacles.*

Under the old covenant, only the physical seed of Abraham or the circumcised converts to Judaism could keep this feast. But a day was coming (and has now come) when the Lord would begin to gather up to Himself the increase of His Seed from *all nations*. Those who refuse to be gathered will experience the plagues and drought that speak of life outside God's provision of Christ.

They Shall Not Appear Before Me Empty-Handed

Perhaps the most important aspect of this ingathering, from the Lord's point of view, is shown to us in the following statement:

Deut 16:16 *"Three times a year all your males shall appear before the Lord your God in the place which He chooses: at the Feast of Unleavened*

Bread, at the Feast of Weeks, and at the Feast of Tabernacles; <u>and they shall not appear before the Lord empty-handed</u>."

To appear before the Lord empty-handed would be for Israel to appear before the Lord bearing nothing of the increase of His Son. We saw this same statement made with reference to the Feast of Unleavened Bread, and indeed the same thing is said with regard to *each* of the feasts. In every feast, God gave Israel a way to relate to Him *in Christ*, a way to offer back to God the work, the merit, and the increase of Christ. As Israel gathered before the Lord three times a year (seven feasts, divided into three groups), I believe *this* was the key idea. Three times a year they were to stand before God, presenting to Him the life, relationship, and increase of His Son.

This is most certainly an important aspect of what God shows us through the Feast of Tabernacles. God provided Israel with His bountiful provision, with His land of promise, and with supernatural growth and increase that was the work of His Spirit. Every year this reality was meant to be recognized by Israel and presented to the Lord as a testimony of the true Harvest of Christ to come.

Deut 16:15 *Seven days you shall keep a sacred feast to the LORD your God in the place which the LORD chooses, <u>because the LORD your God will bless you in all your produce and in all the work of your hands, so that you surely rejoice</u>.*

Just as with many of Christ's parables (i.e. the parable of the sower, the talents, the vineyard), the owner comes and demands the increase of what he had put into his servants' hands. At no point should the servants be found "empty-handed." In the parable of the talents, two of the servants return to their master an increase of what they had been given and were praised for it. The third servant did not lose what the master had given him but was reprimanded for not using it to bring forth an increase. The master says, "You ought to have deposited my money with the bankers, and at my coming I would have received back my own with interest."[83]

We need to understand that even a life devoted to busy Christianity could amount to "empty hands" from the Lord's perspective if the soul of the believer still has nothing of Christ's true increase to offer the Master. God's fruit is the increase of Christ. It may have outward, visible effects in the earth, but the fruit itself is spiritual, internal, and invisible to the natural eye. Very often, man cannot recognize the true fruit of God's Spirit (even as Israel could not recognize their Messiah). Nevertheless, the Farmer always recognizes the increase of His Seed in the soil of our hearts.

The Dwelling Place

The idea of a dwelling place where both God and man dwell together as one is another theme that runs

---

[83] Matthew 25:27

throughout the entire Bible. This dwelling place is shown to us in many scriptures and in many ways to be both something that God has been seeking and planning and also the purpose for which man has been created.

I believe the booths or tabernacles that were set up during this feast speak of our habitation with God. There are some writers who believe that the tabernacles represent our earthly bodies and the fact that our relationship with God is, for a time, experienced in these earthly tents. I have no problem with this idea as long as the focus of this interpretation is *not* upon the earthly tent, but rather upon the living union with God experienced within the tent. It seems more likely, however, that the tabernacles themselves simply represent Christ as our spiritual dwelling place. God took us *out* of one country, kindred, and father's house, and planted us in another—the place He has chosen for His own dwelling place. In the following verse, God shows us that these tabernacles speak of a new dwelling place for those He has taken out of Egypt.

> **Lev 23:42** *You shall dwell in booths for seven days. All who are native Israelites shall dwell in booths,* 43 <u>*that your generations may know that I made the children of Israel dwell in booths when I brought them out of the land of Egypt:*</u> *I am the Lord your God.*

From the very beginning of God's dealing with Israel, He made clear to them that this glorious dwelling place was

His true objective. Immediately after bringing them out of Egypt, the Spirit spoke through Moses, saying,

> **Exod 15:17** *You will bring them in and plant them In the mountain of Your inheritance, In the place, O Lord, which You have made for Your own dwelling, The sanctuary, O Lord, which Your hands have established. 18 "The Lord shall reign forever and ever.*

After entering into covenant with Israel at Sinai, God took Moses up the mountain and revealed to Him the pattern of His spiritual house. Moses was told to build the tabernacle and all of its furnishings exactly according to this pattern because, in every detail, this pattern testified of Christ. Every piece of furniture, curtain, sacrifice, and fragrance had to align perfectly with God's understanding of Jesus Christ, the One by Whom and in Whom man and God would dwell together as one.

> **Exod 25:8** *And let them make Me a sanctuary, that I may dwell among them. 9 According to all that I show you, that is, the pattern of the tabernacle and the pattern of all its furnishings, just so you shall make it.*

Throughout the old covenant age of types and shadows, God spoke of and described His coming eternal dwelling place in a variety of ways. We see it in Exodus 19 as a mountain upon which He descends and into which He invites Israel through the blood of the covenant. We see it in the Tabernacle of Moses in the wilderness and then later in the Temple of Solomon. But even after establishing these natural pictures, He continued to speak through the prophets of an even greater home, a resting place where He would be eternally joined to His people.

> ***Isa 66:1*** *Thus says the LORD: "Heaven is My throne, And earth is My footstool. <u>Where is the house that you will build Me? And where is the place of My rest?</u> 2 For all those things My hand has made, And all those things exist," says the Lord. "But on this one will I look: On him who is poor and of a contrite spirit, And who trembles at My word.*

> ***Ezek 37:26*** *Moreover I will make a covenant of peace with them, and it shall be an everlasting covenant with them; I will establish them and multiply them, and <u>I will set My sanctuary in their midst forevermore</u>. 27 My tabernacle also shall be with them; indeed I will be their God, and they shall be My people. 28 The nations also will know that I, the LORD, sanctify Israel, <u>when My sanctuary is in their midst forevermore</u>.*

The Consummation of God's Plan for Israel

With the combination of these two elements of Tabernacles—the ingathering of the harvest and the dwelling place of God—we have an incredible picture given to us of the end and purpose towards which God is steering His new creation. As we have seen, deliverance from sin and death was not Israel's purpose. They were delivered *for* a purpose, and that purpose is shown to us in this final feast.

John 14–17 seems to focus on these same two realities. In these chapters, Jesus is speaking with His disciples and praying to His Father on the eve of His crucifixion. In His last moments before the cross, God's true harvest and eternal dwelling place seem to have been foremost on Jesus' mind. In John 15, the focus is the increase of Christ by way of the "branches" that are joined to Him and abide in Him. This is the true fruit that glorifies the Father.

> *John 15:1 I am the true vine, and My Father is the vinedresser. 2 Every branch in Me that does not bear fruit He takes away; and every branch that bears fruit He prunes, that it may bear more fruit... 4 Abide in Me, and I in you. As the branch cannot bear fruit of itself, unless it abides in the vine, neither can you, unless you abide in Me. 8 By this My Father is glorified, that you bear much fruit.*

In chapters 14, 16, and 17, Jesus had so much to say about the Father's house, the eternal habitation where God and man come to live as one.

> *John 14:20 At that day you will know that I am in My Father, and you in Me, and I in you.*

John 17:24 *Father, I desire that they also whom You gave Me may be with Me where I am... I in them, and You in Me; that they may be made perfect in one...that they all may be one, as You, Father, are in Me, and I in You; that they also may be one in Us.*

Conclusion

My hope is that the reader sees in these seven feasts so much more than laws and ceremonies and religion. I believe that here we have a precious God-given picture of His eternal purpose for all who come to life in His Son. In the Feasts of Israel, God has shared with us His view of the journey of Jesus Christ from a single dying seed to a multi-membered, resurrected harvest.

Made in the USA
Charleston, SC
19 January 2015